Parents and School Violence

Answers that Reveal Essential Steps for Improving Schools

Gerard Giordano

ROWMAN & LITTLEFIELD
Lanham • Boulder • New York • London

Published by Rowman & Littlefield
An imprint of The Rowman & Littlefield Publishing Group, Inc.
4501 Forbes Boulevard, Suite 200, Lanham, Maryland 20706
www.rowman.com

86-90 Paul Street, London EC2A 4NE

British Library Cataloguing in Publication Information Available

Library of Congress Cataloging-in-Publication Data

Names: Giordano, Gerard, author.
Title: Parents and school violence : answers that reveal essential steps for improving schools / Gerard Giordano.
Description: Lanham : Rowman & Littlefield Publishers, [2022] | Includes bibliographical references. | Summary: "This book explores advice about controlling school violence"-- Provided by publisher.
Identifiers: LCCN 2022011987 (print) | LCCN 2022011988 (ebook) | ISBN 9781475861709 (paperback) | ISBN 9781475861716 (ebook)
Subjects: LCSH: School violence--Prevention. | Education--Parent participation. | School improvement programs. | School management and organization.
Classification: LCC LB3013.3 .G56 2022 (print) | LCC LB3013.3 (ebook) | DDC 371.7/82--dc23/eng/20220425
LC record available at https://lccn.loc.gov/2022011987
LC ebook record available at https://lccn.loc.gov/2022011988

∞™ The paper used in this publication meets the minimum requirements of American National Standard for Information Sciences—Permanence of Paper for Printed Library Materials, ANSI/NISO Z39.48-1992.

This book is based on classroom conversations with my students. It comprises my words but their thoughts.

Contents

Preface

What Is the Best Way to Deal with School Violence?

A student asked me, "Are we going to die today?"

—Florida High School Teacher Ivy Schamis, 2020

[The] mayor appears asleep at the wheel on crime.

—Florida High School Student Jack Rowan, 2020

[School] signs . . . that read "this is a gun-free zone" . . . are in effect inviting the bad guys.

—Florida Letter-to-the-Editor Writer Cilla Whitcher, 2019

If someone walks onto this [school's] campus, they're going to be shot and killed.

—Florida School Principal Bill Jones, 2019

[Some schools have security plans] held together with nothing more than chewing gum, duct tape and hope.

—Florida Grand Jury, 2020

[The origin of school shootings] is not what's happening within school walls, but the communities.

—Florida School Board Member Warren Jones, 2020

A Miami teenager had been expelled from his high school for fighting. He returned to that school in 2018, pulled out a gun, and attacked students and staff. He killed seventeen of them and injured others.

Parents worried that additional attacks would follow the one in Miami. They wanted to know how to prevent them. They also wanted to know how to intervene should they still occur.

The parents posed their questions to the persons who were responsible for keeping students safe. They went to teachers, principals, police officers, security consultants, and elected officials.

These groups agreed that specialized safety devices could be useful. They believed that highly trained safety personnel could also be useful.

The groups did not agree on all points. For example, they disagreed about the amount that they should spend on safety devices. Some preferred pricey devices, such as facial recognition software. Others were satisfied with much less expensive devices, such as bulletproof vests.

The groups also disagreed about the type of personnel that would be needed to keep students safe. Some recommended therapeutic personnel, such as counselors, psychologists, and social workers. Others recommended emergency-intervention personnel, such as police officers, armed resource officers, and gun-carrying teachers.

The parents had asked how to protect children at school. They were frustrated by the different answers they received. They resolved that they would answer this question for themselves.

FEATURES

This book explores recommendations to control school violence. It looks at student arrests, active shooter drills, panic buttons, emergency texting, armed school personnel, facial recognition software, restorative justice programs, anti-bullying programs, zero-tolerance policies, mental health counseling, mandatory psychiatric screening, therapeutic yoga, police dogs, bulletproof backpacks, and bans on rap music.

The chapters in this book rely on a distinctive type of problem solving. They begin with a problem outside the schools, follow with a problem inside the schools, and conclude with side-by-side analyses. They help readers see how one problem can contain a key to solving the other.

SERIES

This book is part of a series about the enormous impact that parents have had on education. Previous books in this series have focused on tests, textbooks, and school technology.

AUDIENCE

This book is intended for a general audience. It will be especially engaging to parents. However, it also is intended for educators and professionals in school-related fields.

Acknowledgements

This book is a tribute to my remarkable editor—Tom Koerner. His suggestions, always posed in a calm and probing manner, have had an extraordinary impact on this book . . . and on me as an author.

Chapter 1

How Effective Is Police-Expedited Expulsion?

No, don't put handcuffs on . . . me!

—Officer-Detained Student Kaia Rolle, 2020

Arresting a teenager takes an officer [away from patrolling for] . . . about three hours.

—*Florida Times-Union* Editorial Board, 2020

[School] districts that have gotten along without police officers should think twice before deploying them.

—*New York Times* Editorial Board, 2013

Placing officers in the schools . . . [pushes] kids into the criminal system.

—Criminology Professor Denise Gottfredson, 2013

Keep police out of schools . . . [because] kids will do better without them.

—Criminology Professors James Fox and Aviva Rich-Shea, 2020

Professors at Evergreen State College organized an annual event during which they directed minority persons to stay home. They intended to foster racial tolerance. They later reorganized the event and directed nonminority persons to stay home. They assumed that this change would foster even greater tolerance. They were surprised by the consequences.

Educational administrators expelled students from school. They intended to foster safety. They later hired police officers to expedite the process. They assumed that this change would foster even greater safety. They were surprised by the consequences.

EXPELLING PROFESSORS

Legislators in the state of Washington authorized a new public college during the late 1960s. They then selected a group of founders. They directed them to select a name, pick a site, and take the steps that were necessary for the institution to become fully operational.

The founders embraced the challenges. They assigned a name for the school—Evergreen State College. They also assigned a site—Olympia. They then constructed buildings, hired faculty, and recruited students. They beamed when classes began in 1967.

The founders had one additional challenge: they were to ensure that Evergreen State College had a distinctive mission. They left this responsibility to the administrators and faculty.

The administrators and faculty wanted their school to have a distinctive academic mission. They devised an unusual approach for designing curricula. They furnished their students with an ever-changing menu of courses. They then allowed them to decide which courses they would take.

The administrators and faculty had an unusual approach to designing curricula. They complemented it with an equally unusual approach to assigning grades. They used narrative descriptions rather than letter grades to document students' scholastic achievements.

The administrators and faculty took pride in their distinctive academic mission. They took equal pride in their distinctive political mission. They pledged that they would promote social justice and encourage students to follow their example.

The administrators and faculty anticipated that they would attract students. They were quite successful. By 2017, they had drawn four thousand of them.

The professors attempted to find exciting ways to promote their commitment to social justice. As an example, they organized an annual "day of absence" on which they encouraged minority persons to stay away from campus. They told them that their absence would make the entire campus appreciate their contributions.

The Evergreen professors believed that the day of absence was meaningful. Nonetheless, they looked for a way to make it even more meaningful. They had a novel idea in 2017.

The professors announced that they were changing the event's format: they were now directing all minority persons to come to campus but urging all nonminority persons to stay at home. They assumed that these changes would help the nonminority persons better understand the distressing experiences that minority persons had endured during the era of segregation.

Enthusiasts

The professors were eager to see how students would react to the changes that they had made. They contacted minority students on their campus.

Some of the minority students had expressed dissatisfaction with prevailing racial attitudes at Evergreen. They believed that the changes to the day of absence might improve those attitudes. They supported the changes.

The professors who had organized the changes were pleased with the way minority students reacted. They noted that many of minority faculty reacted in the same fashion. They then turned their attention to nonminority faculty.

Nonminority faculty members were supportive. Nonetheless, not every one of them was supportive. A biology professor created a stir by writing a public letter questioning the changes.

Some students were upset with this biology professor. They looked for a way to show their displeasure. They disrupted his classes.

The protesters expected the professor to recant his views. They were disappointed when he refused. They therefore met with the college's president. They urged him to expel the biology professor from campus. They threatened to escalate the disruption if he did not comply.

The president worried that the professor might be endangered by the angry students. He therefore directed him to move his classes to an off-campus site.

Skeptics

The professors who had made changes to the day of absence were concerned about their impact on students. They assumed that the event was giving them valuable insights about racism. They were pleased.

The professors were also concerned about journalists. They were aware that they had an immense impact on the parents of current and prospective students. They depended on the parents to supply the tuition and fees for their children.

The journalists had supported the original day of absence. They viewed the event as an important way to raise awareness of racial discrimination. They also supported the 2017 changes to it. They viewed them as attempts to make the original event even more potent. However, they were concerned about some of the disruptive events associated with the changes.

Conservative journalists, such as those associated with *FOX News*, were especially scornful of the changes. They accused the progressive professors of encouraging Evergreen's students to stage the protests against the dissenting professor.

Politically progressive journalists had attitudes that were different from those of their conservative counterparts. For example, the journalists at the *New York Times* emphasized the good intentions of the campus activists. However, even they became dismayed when the activists demanded that their college president refrain from using hand gestures because they interpreted these as threats.

Parents of students already at Evergreen recognized that this school had nontraditional curricula, grading policies, and an extremely high-profile commitment to social justice. Even though they regretted the negative publicity that the school had attracted after it ousted a professor, they still discerned its remarkable attributes. Most of them encouraged their children to remain enrolled and pursue their degrees.

The parents of prospective students discerned Evergreen's many positive attributes. They respected the ways in which it had handled instruction, curriculum, and grading. They also respected the way it had supported progressive social causes.

The parents of prospective students were concerned about only one aspect of Evergreen—the groups that were feuding on its campus. Because of this concern, they decided to send their children to campuses with less tumult. They predicted that other parents would agree with them and that they would cause the enrollment at the college to decline steeply. They were correct.

EXPELLING STUDENTS

Educational administrators in public schools were concerned about troublesome students. They realized that they might prevent their peers from learning. They realized that they might even endanger them.

The administrators looked for strategies to control troublesome students. They relied heavily on punishments.

Some of the administrators preferred moderate punishments. As examples, they detained troublesome students after school, barred them from social events, or excluded them from sports.

Some of the administrators were disappointed with the minimal impact of moderate punishments. They preferred more severe ones. As examples, they publicly humiliated students, sent them to weekend detention, or paddled them.

Some administrators were disappointed even with the severe punishments. They still had one more option—they could expel troublesome students from school.

The administrators used expulsion as a disciplinary strategy. For example, they tried to change the behaviors of students who were continually disruptive in class. They also used it to change the behaviors of those students who were habitually truant.

However, in addition to using it as a disciplinary tool, the administrators also used explusion as a safety strategy. For example, they expelled students who fought with peers or who brought weapons to school.

The educational administrators in Miami were particularly eager to find effective strategies for dealing with troublesome students. They had been horrified in 2018 after a teenager brought a gun to school and killed seventeen students and staff.

The administrators in Miami were in a difficult situation. They struggled to explain how a student could kill seventeen persons. They also struggled to explain why security personnel had trouble intervening. Finally, they struggled to explain how they would prevent an event of this sort from recurring.

The Miami administrators were not the only ones who had to deal with dangerous students in 2018. Three percent of the nation's administrators reported that they had to deal with armed students that year.

Most of the educational administrators used the same strategy to deal with armed students: they expelled them. Nonetheless, they conceded that this strategy sometimes failed. They noted that it had failed in Miami, where an assailant had been expelled from Marjory Stoneman High School but then returned with arms to that campus.

The administrators had confidence in expulsion. However, they needed to adapt it. They needed a group of professionals who would help them expel students. They already had police officers on their campuses. They could enlist their services. Nonetheless, they still wanted to hire more officers.

The administrators did recruit and hire additional police officers to assist those already on their campuses. They directed them to patrol school buildings and grounds, identify troublesome students, arrest them, and steer them into the juvenile criminal justice system.

Enthusiasts

The educational administrators were excited. They believed that the hiring of additional police officers would enable them to expedite expulsions. They hoped that other persons would share their excitement. They especially hoped that parents would be enthusiastic.

Some parents were enthusiastic about bringing police officers into schools. They hoped that they would prevent troublesome students from harming their classmates.

The supportive parents assumed that the police officers would be able to handle troublesome students. However, they did have a concern. They wondered whether the police would be able to gain the trust of well-behaved students.

The school administrators assured the parents that the officers would be trained to develop rapport with the well-behaved students. They predicted that they quickly would earn their trust.

Skeptics

Some parents were excited by the prospect of having police officers help expel troublesome students. Others were not.

The skeptics doubted that the officers could win children's trust. They noted that the officers who patrolled their neighborhoods had been trained about how to deal with children but still had been too aggressive with them.

The skeptical parents predicted that police would continue to be aggressive at school. Nonetheless, they had to wait until the officers were deployed before they could gather the data that they would need to confirm this prediction.

The skeptical parents eventually did gather data. They then examined the categories of students whom the officers had been arresting. They noted that they had been arresting a disproportionately high number of minority teens at the high schools. They suspected that they had been profiling these students based on race.

The skeptical parents found another troublesome pattern with the officers. They observed them arresting a disproportionate number of students with disabilities at the high schools. They suspected that they had misinterpreted the reluctance of these students to make eye contact or to answer questions as signs of defiance. They noted that they were repeating this pattern even when they were dealing with young students who had disabilities.

The administrators listened respectfully to the parents' comments about school-based officers. They were concerned about their views. However, they also were concerned about students' views.

The students, like their parents, had mixed reactions to the officers. Some students supported them. They hoped that the officers would protect them from violent peers.

Although some students were supportive of the officers, others were skeptical. The skeptical students explained that aggressive officers had arrested them, their siblings, or their friends and pushed them into the juvenile criminal justice system. They concluded that these officers posed too much of a threat to remain in their schools.

RESPONDING TO QUESTIONS ABOUT EXPULSION

Four questions are contained in this section. They focus on two case studies.

The first case study concerned professors at Evergreen State College. These professors organized an annual event during which they directed minority persons to stay home. They intended to foster racial tolerance. Later, the Evergreen professors reorganized the event and directed nonminority persons to stay home. They assumed that this change would foster even greater tolerance. However, they were surprised by the consequences.

While the first case study in this chapter concerned professors, the next one focused on educational administrators. The administrators expelled troublesome students from school. They intended to foster safety. Later, the administrators hired police officers to help expel troublesome students. They assumed that this change would foster even greater safety. However, they were surprised by the consequences.

The questions at the end of this chapter will assist you if are going through this book on your own. The questions at the ends of subsequent chapters have the same characteristic. They provide opportunities to simulate participation in college classrooms where professors are using the case method.

Professors who use the case method direct students to examine several related incidents. They are not surprised if the students do not detect similarities between the incidents. They then follow up with questions that guide them through their analyses.

Although the following questions will help you if you are going through this book on your own, they also will help you if you are going through it while participating in actual college courses.

Question 1: Why Did Professors Encourage Minority Persons to Stay Home during a Campus Event?

The professors at Evergreen State College organized an annual event during which they directed minority persons to stay home. They intended to foster racial tolerance.

How did different groups respond to the professors? Focus on two groups: students and parents.

Did the students have low confidence, moderate confidence, or high confidence in the way that the professors were behaving? How did their parents feel? Explain the bases for your answers.

When answering these questions, as well as those that follow, you can rely on the information in this chapter. You also might rely on some of the sources that are identified in the references at the rear of the book. If you are reading this chapter with colleagues, you are encouraged to converse with them about the best way to answer the questions.

Question 2: Why Did Professors Later Encourage Nonminority Persons to Stay Home during a Campus Event?

The professors at Evergreen State College later reorganized their annual event by directing nonminority persons to stay home. They assumed that this change would foster even greater racial tolerance.

How did different groups respond to the professors? Focus on two groups: students and parents.

Did the students have low confidence, moderate confidence, or high confidence in the way that the professors were behaving? How did their parents feel? Explain the bases for your answers.

Question 3: Why Did Educational Administrators Expel Students from School?

Educational administrators expelled dangerous students from their schools. They intended to foster safety.

How did diverse groups respond to these educational administrators? Focus on two groups: students and parents.

Did the students have low confidence, moderate confidence, or high confidence in the way that the educational administrators were behaving? How did the parents feel? Explain the bases for your answers.

Question 4: Why Did Educational Administrators Later Hire Police Officers to Help Expel Students?

Educational administrators later hired police officers to help them expel dangerous students. They assumed that this change would foster greater safety.

How did diverse groups respond to these educational administrators? Focus on two groups: students and parents.

Did the students have low confidence, moderate confidence, or high confidence in the way that the educational administrators were behaving? How did the parents feel? Explain the bases for your answers.

SUMMARY

Professors at Evergreen State College organized an annual event during which they directed minority persons to stay home. They intended to foster racial tolerance. They later reorganized the event and directed nonminority persons to stay home. They assumed that this change would foster even greater tolerance. They were surprised by some of the consequences.

Educational administrators expelled students from school. They intended to foster safety. They later hired police officers to expedite the expulsion process. They assumed that this change would foster even greater safety. They were surprised by some of the consequences.

Chapter 2

How Effective Are Shocking Videos?

[Our] students are . . . introduced to . . . safety . . . . training videos [about how to evacuate classrooms or barricade them].

—Bethel School District, 2016

[A] video is being shown to . . . [our] 6–12 graders . . . [to explain] Secured Perimeter, Shelter in Place, Evacuation, Room Clear and Lockdown.

—Littleton Public Schools, 2020

You have to educate these kids on how to be safe but you . . . don't want to create hysteria and anxiety.

—Schoolboard Member Patrick Canan, 2019

The number of developmentally uninformed, child-uninformed and completely stupid ideas [about how to increase school safety] is mind-numbing.

—ChildTrauma Academy Director Bruce Perry, 2019

Political candidates looked for ways to influence voters. They tried to win them over by exposing them to conventional videos about themselves and their opponents. However, to make a greater impact, they later turned to using more shocking videos.

School administrators looked for ways to influence students. They tried to keep them safe by exposing them to conventional videos about active shooters. However, to make a greater imact, they too later turned to using more shocking videos.

SHOCKING POLITICAL VIDEOS

Filmmakers historically had made movies that comprised only real-life persons and real-life scenes. However, they later acquired the ability to create computer-generated images (CGIs).

Some filmmakers relied exclusively on real-life persons and scenes. Others relied only on CGI images. Still others combined the two approaches: they made live-image recordings but then inserted CGI images into them.

Martin Scorsese created a sensation with a film that he released in 2019. He hired famous actors to portray the lead characters in the *The Irishman*. However, he used CGI technology to change their appearance. He made the actors, who were in their late seventies, appear as they did when they were fifty years younger.

Scorsese highlighted use of CGI technology to "de-age" actors who were in their senior years. He hoped that the novelty of the technique would impress film critics and viewers.

Scorsese did make an impression on film critics and viewers. He also made one on political candidates.

The political candidates had been searching for a way to increase their odds of winning elections. They had been relying heavily on video advertisements. They commissioned some advertisements that highlighted their personal qualifications for elected office. They commissioned others that emphasized their opponents' deficiencies.

The candidates asked videographers if they could increase the impact of their advertisements. They were excited by the suggestions that they made.

The videographers offered to use CGI technology to alter film clips for the candidates who hired them. They explained that they could make them appear extremely poised and coherent.

The videographers also offered to emphasize the negative image of the hiring candidates' political opponents. They explained that they could make them appear extremely confused and inarticulate.

The videographers told their clients that they had additional ways to alter films. For example, they could erase participants from videos. They also could introduce new participants into them. They only needed instructions from their clients.

Enthusiasts

The videographers created samples of CGI-manipulated videos. They then released them on the Internet to gauge how viewers reacted to them.

Viewers were fascinated by the videos. Journalists were especially intrigued by them. The journalists referred to them with a clever term: deep fake videos. They warned that only experts could determine whether videos were genuine or deep fakes.

Although deep fake videos may have relied on sophisticated technology, many of them had absurd premises. Some of those that depicted President Trump were patently absurd. For example, one video superimposed the president's face onto the torso of a professional wrestler. In this case, the president stated that the video was hilarious.

Another deep fake video showed Nancy Pelosi, the Democratic Speaker of the House, making remarks to an audience. It used CGI to slow down her oral cadence. Ms. Pelosi slammed this video for making her seem inebriated.

In some cases, the culprits behind the deep fake videos could be traced. In most cases, they were unidentifiable.

Skeptics

Candidates who commissioned deep fake videos paid attention to the impact they had on journalists. However, they were more interested in the impact they had on voters.

The voters had mixed reactions. They supported deep fake videos when their use benefitted the candidates for whom they intended to vote. They opposed them when they benefitted those candidates for whom they did not intend to vote.

The candidates were not surprised by the way that partisan voters were reacting to deep fake videos. However, they wondered how independent voters were reacting to them. They realized that this group was critical during elections.

Some independent voters found the deep fake videos offensive. Some found them entertaining. Few found them persuasive.

SHOCKING SCHOOL VIDEOS

Parents expected administrators to look after their children at school. They asked them to report the steps they were taking to keep them safe.

The educational administrators were prepared for this question. They explained that they had given teachers greater safety responsibilities.

The educational administrators had hired security consultants to train the teachers about how to handle life-threatening situations. They had directed them to demonstrate how teachers could create safe classroom environments, how they could communicate critical safety information to students, and how they should respond during safety crises.

The educational administrators supplemented the training with safety videos. Some of them acquired these videos from their state department of education or school safety advocacy groups. Others hired businesspeople to custom design videos for their school districts.

The educational administrators were pleased with the training videos they had shown to teachers. They searched for additional videos to show to students. They hoped that these videos would instruct the students about the warning signs of danger, the steps they should take if they detected those signs, and the steps that they should take should they become involved in life-threatening crises.

The administrators were interested in student safety videos on a full range of topics. For example, they wanted ones that explained how students could be safe while crossing streets, riding school buses, dining in cafeterias, and socializing on schoolgrounds. However, they had a special interest in ones that explained how to be safe when confronted by active shooters.

The administrators experimented with safety videos that had a subdued tone. However, they questioned whether these videos were having a major impact. They reckoned that they needed to be more engrossing—and shocking.

The administrators went back to the businesspeople and safety advocacy groups to request their assistance. They were pleased when both parties said that they could develop videos that were realistic, engrossing, and shocking.

The new videos were extremely explicit. They showed armed assailants menacing students. They then challenged the viewers to specify whether the students in the films should flee, hide, or fight.

Enthusiasts

The administrators directed teachers to show the shocking videos to their students. They directed teachers to keep an eye on how their students reacted.

The students could not help but be engrossed by the realistic videos. At the same time, they were extermely frightened by them.

Many students viewed the videos as valuable. Even those who were frightened believed that the videos prepared them to deal with active shooters. They concluded that although the footage was disturbing, it contained information that could save their lives.

Skeptics

The school administrators kept an eye on parents as well as students.

The parents had reactions to the videos that were like those of their children. They noted that the videos had frightened their children. Nonetheless, many believed that they still could be beneficial.

Other parents were skeptical. They believed that the shocking videos were causing unreasonable psychological and emotional damage. They wanted them removed from their children's schools.

RESPONDING TO QUESTIONS ABOUT DISCONCERTING VIDEOS

Candidates looked for a way to influence voters during elections. They used conventional videos to highlight their own strengths and their opponents' weaknesses. However, to make a greater impact, they later turned to using more shocking videos.

Educational administrators looked for a way to influence students at school. They used conventional videos to prepare them to respond to active shooters. However, to make a greater impact, they too later turned to using more shocking videos.

Attempts to influence voters and students were unrelated. Nonetheless, they had some similarities. After you answer the following questions, see if you discern those similarities.

Question 1: Why Did Candidates Use Conventional Videos?

Candidates incorporated conventional videos into their political campaigns. They hoped that they would highlight their own strengths and their opponents' weaknesses.

How did different groups respond to the candidates? Focus on two groups: voters who affiliated with the same political party as the candidates and voters who did not affiliate with the same political party as the candidates.

Did voters who affiliated with the same political party as the candidates have low confidence, moderate confidence, or high confidence in the way the candidates were behaving? How did independent voters feel? Explain the bases for your answers.

When answering these questions, as well as those that follow, you can rely on the information in this chapter. You also might rely on some of the sources that are identified in the references at the rear of the book. If you are reading this chapter with colleagues, you are encouraged to converse with them about the best way to answer the questions.

Question 2: Why Did Candidates Turn to Shocking Videos?

The candidates judged that conventional videos had limited impact on voters. They believed that shocking videos would more effectively highlight their own strengths and their opponents' weaknesses.

How did different groups respond to the candidates? Focus on two groups: voters who affiliated with the same political party as the candidates and independent voters.

Did the voters who affiliated with the same political party as the candidates have low confidence, moderate confidence, or high confidence in the way that the candidates were behaving? How did independent voters feel? Explain the bases for your answers.

Question 3: Why Did Educational Administrators Use Conventional Safety Videos?

Educational administrators incorporated conventional videos into their school safety plans. They hoped that they would prepare students to respond to active shooters.

How did diverse groups respond to these educational administrators? Focus on two groups: students and their parents.

Did the students have low confidence, moderate confidence, or high confidence in the way that the educational administrators were behaving? How did their parents feel? Explain the bases for your answers.

Question 4: Why Did Educational Administrators Turn to Shocking Videos?

The educational administrators judged that conventional videos had limited impact on students. They believed that shocking videos would more effectively prepare students to respond to active shooters.

How did diverse groups respond to these educational administrators? Focus on two groups: students and their parents.

Did the students have low confidence, moderate confidence, or high confidence in the way that the educational administrators were behaving? How did their parents feel? Explain the bases for your answers.

SUMMARY

Political candidates looked for ways to influence voters. They used conventional videos to highlight their own strengths and their opponents' weaknesses. However, to make a greater impact, they later turned to using more shocking videos.

Educational administrators looked for ways to influence students. They used conventional videos to prepare them to respond to active shooters. However, to make a greater impact, they too later turned to using more shocking videos

Chapter 3

How Effective Are Bulletproof Backpacks?

[Our company's bulletproof backpack] looks like a regular backpack.

—Guard Dog Security Firm, 2020

[Our company's bulletproof backpacks] provide instant protection from handgun attacks.

—ArmorMe Security Firm, 2018

[I gave my son a bulletproof backpack because] I want [him] to be able to come home from school.

—Ohio Parent John Drury, 2019

47% of parents show interest in bulletproof backpacks.

—Polling Spokesperson Kasey Meredith, 2019

[Bulletproof backpacks give] a false sense of security . . . . [and are] a waste of money.

—Unidentified North Carolina Parent, 2019

Executives paid advertising firms to promote Nike running shoes. However, they also prodded the executives at competing companies to inadvertently promote them. They paid billions of dollars in one case; they paid nothing in the other.

School administrators paid security firms for safety devices. However, they also prodded parents to furnish them at their own expense. They paid billions of dollars in one case; they paid nothing in the other.

NO-COST MARKETING

The executives at the major running shoe corporations searched for novel ways to sell products. They were phenomenally successful. They increased sales to more than thirteen billion dollars annually.

The executives at different running shoe firms shared a common interest in expanding their market. However, they competed against each other to make sure that their firm had the largest possible share of that market.

Asics, Adidas, and Nike were the leaders among the running shoe corporations. They effectively controlled the market. Asics had fifteen percent of the market while Adidas had six percent. However, Nike was the dominant firm, with more than fifty percent of the market.

The executives at Nike were proud that they dominated the running shoe market. They had achieved this prominence by making fashionable shoes, getting top athletes to endorse them, and advertising them extensively. They spent billions of dollars annually on these strategies.

The Nike executives had one more strategy to which they were committed. In fact, they believed that this last strategy had elevated Nike above its competitors.

The Nike executives invested heavily in product development. They made sure that their shoes incorporated the latest performance technology. They hired athletic doctors, trainers, and technicians to assist them.

Although they spent vast amounts on product development, the Nike executives discerned only incremental advancements of their running shoes every year. They believed that this made sense because they already had the most advanced shoes in the world.

The Nike executives became extremely excited in 2017. They were informed that their research team had a truly revolutionary product.

The researchers had developed a new high-performance foam. They noted that it had more spring than the foam in Nike's best running shoes. They calculated that this spring was eighty-seven percent efficient in pushing back after it was depressed. They contrasted this with Nike's current foam, which was only sixty-five percent efficient.

The researchers had fashioned a shoe sole from the new foam and then molded it to a carbon liner. This combination created stability without decreasing the foam's flexibility or bounce. They then attached the new sole to a running shoe.

The researchers distributed their revolutionary shoes to amateur runners. They also distributed them to world-class runners. They asked them to keep track of their running times with the new shoes and compare them to their times with current shoes. They were ebullient after both groups reported that they ran faster.

The executives believed that their new shoe would significantly increase the running speeds of athletes. They were ready to begin selling it. However, they needed a name for it. They consulted with their marketers.

The marketers coined an obstruse name—the *Vaporfly*. They assured the executives that this name would be trendy.

The executives accepted this advice. They called the shoe the Vaporfly. However, they also had to decide on a price. They again called on their marketers.

The marketers noted that most runners purchased shoes priced at one-hundred and twenty-five dollars. They encouraged the executives to set the price of the Vaporfly at twice that amount. They were confident that the new shoe would generate enough buzz to justify this price.

Enthusiasts

The Nike executives were excited about their new product. They hoped that runners would share their enthusiasm. They distributed Vaporfly shoes at no cost to a large group comprising professional runners and elite college runners. They were eager to see the athletes' reactions.

The athletes who received Vaporfly shoes were directed to make two runs at their top speed. They were to complete one run with their current shoes. They were to complete the second with the Vaporfly. They then were to compare the results.

The athletes were astounded by the results. They ran four percent faster with the Vaporfly.

Some of the elite athletes were excited after the experiments. Those who had signed contracts with Nike could not wait to compete in events at which they would wear the Vaporfly.

Some elite athletes were unnerved after their experiments. These athletes had signed contracts with firms other than Nike. As a result, they could not wear the Vaporfly during competitions. They had to wear the brand of shoe from their sponsor. They worried that they would be at a disadvantage.

The disconcerted athletes were particularly worried about the Olympics that had been scheduled for 2020. They appealed to their sponsors—the firms that were competing against Nike for sales.

The executives at the competing firms demanded that the International Olympics Committee (IOC) ban the Vaporfly. They contended that persons who wore this new shoe would have an enormous advantage over competitors. They compared that advantage to pharmaceutical doping.

Skeptics

Journalists quickly learned about Vaporfly. They were interested because it was reputed to significantly increase running speed. They questioned whether this claim was accurate.

The journalists contacted the professional athletes and college athletes who had made testimonials. They assumed that they had been misquoted. They were surprised when all of them stood by their testimonials.

The journalists were still doubtful. They therefore contacted sports scientists at universities. They searched out those who had been carefully monitoring running shoe performance. They asked them to investigate the claims about the Vaporfly. They expected them to dispute them. They were shocked when they instead verified them.

The journalists had contacted professional athletes, college athletes, and sports scientists. They were impressed by their uniform praise for the Vaporfly. However, they still wished to contact one more group—the executives at competing running shoe firms. They asked whether the new shoe was truly the revolutionary product that Nike had been publicizing.

The executives at competing firms did not question the performance claims about the Vaporfly. In fact, they had asked the International Olympic Committee (IOC) to ban this shoe precisely because they believed the claims. Many still stood by that request.

Some of the executives regretted their request for an IOC ban. They explained that they had been tricked into making it. They had not realized that their request would supply the Vaporfly with a boundless trove of free publicity.

The regretful executives had tried to block Nike from grabbing an even larger share of the running shoe market. They concluded that that they inadvertently had assisted their competitor.

NO-COST SCHOOL SAFETY

Parents questioned whether their children were safe at school. They demanded that they be protected.

Parents in Florida were especially alert to school safety. They had been unnerved by the incidents at a Miami-area high school in 2018. A former pupil entered his school, unpacked a weapon, and assaulted students and staff. He killed seventeen of them and injured another seventeen.

The parents worried that the events in Miami would be replicated in other communities across their state. They demanded that educational administrators take preventative steps.

The educational administrators assured the parents that they had taken some preventative steps. They also assured parents that they were considering a full range of additional steps.

The educational administrators were considering hiring special safety personnel, such as armed officers, school resource officers, and school guardians. They also were considering purchases of special safety equipment, such as metal detectors, surveillance cameras, facial recognition software, and remotely activated door locks. They even were considering the leasing of special dogs who were trained to detect weapons.

The educational administrators agreed that they needed to take special safety measures. However, they disagreed among themselves about the specific measures that they should implement to keep students safe. Some of them preferred the personnel. Others preferred the equipment. Still others preferred the dogs.

The educational administrators examined the benefits of safety measures. They also examined their costs. For example, they noted that armed officers had clear benefits. They also noted that they were extremely expensive. Some were not sure that they could afford them.

Florida's educational administrators turned to parents for feedback. They told them that they wanted the most effective safety measures. However, they were in a quandary because they had limited funds.

Many parents urged the administrators to hire personnel. They believed that they should seek individuals who were experienced, trained, and armed. They preferred police officers. However, they might settle for school resource officers (SROs). They noted that the governor and state legislators had provided funding to cover the cost of safety personnel.

The administrators acknowledged that they had state-supplied funds for school police officers or SROs. However, they did not have the full amount that they would need. For this reason, they were on the lookout for a cheap way to get safety personnel onto school campuses.

When the educational administrators made decisions about safety personnel, they considered two factors: effectiveness and cost. When they made decisions about safety devices, they considered the same two factors.

The administrators were interested in safety devices that were effective. As examples, they had confidence in facial recognition software and remotely activated door locks. However, they also considered their cost, which was high.

The administrators were especially interested in safety devices that were cheap as well as effective. Ideally, they hoped to find some that were cost-free. They were excited when they heard about transparent backpacks.

Educational administrators had been recommending transparent backpacks for years. Some of they had made them mandatory in their schools. They then were able to inspect the items in their students' backpacks. They then confiscated any items that were dangerous.

Proponents believed that X-ray machines and transparent backpacks had the same benefits. However, they noted that the X-ray machines were purchased by schools while the transparent backpacks were purchased by parents.

The administrators at Marjory Stoneman Douglas High School listened attentively to the debate about transparent backpacks. They realized that their school had been the site for an internationally publicized school shooting. They concluded that transparent backpacks might prevent another shooting.

The administrators at Marjory Stoneman Douglas High School told parents that they would be requiring students to carry transparent backpacks. They added that they then would be inspecting these packs for dangerous items.

Enthusiasts

The school administrators kept their eyes on the governor and their state legislators. They realized that they had insisted on an SRO in every school.

The governor and legislators reiterated their mandate. They still insisted on SROs in all schools. They were annoyed at those educational administrators who resisted them.

Some of the noncompliant administrators had said that they did not want any guns in their schools, even if they were in the hands of highly trained SROs. Others, who thanked the elected officials for additional safety funding, still could not afford SROs. Both groups wanted to substitute cheaper alternatives, such as the transparent backpacks.

The elected officials objected to transparent backpacks when they substituted for SROs. However, they had no objection to them when they complemented SROs, as they did at Marjory Stoneman Douglas High School.

The school administrators were interested in the response from elected officials to transparent backpacks. However, they were just as interested in the response from parents.

Some of the parents approved of the transparent backpacks. They realized that they would have to pay for them. However, they were not disconcerted by their prices, which were not that much more than those of standard backpacks. They told the administrators that they were willing to buy them for their children if they would keep them safe.

Skeptics

Some parents were not particularly interested in transparent backpacks. They doubted that busy school staff members would find the time to inspect the items in them. They predicted that even those who did inspect them might still fail to discern knives and small handguns.

The skeptics believed that backpacks still could play a critical role in school safety. They explained that they were not interested in backpacks fashioned from flimsy transparent plastic; they wanted ones made of bulletproof material.

The parents identified the diverse ways in which children could deploy bulletproof backpacks. If they placed them in front of their chests, they would have armored vests. If they placed them on their backs, they would have protection while fleeing. If they placed them on the floor, they would have bulletproof shields behind which to cower. If they connected several of them, they would have tent-like zones under which to be safe.

The educational administrators listened respectfully to the parents. They assured them that they would investigate bulletproof backpacks.

The educational administrators discovered that some bulletproof backpacks would stop handgun rounds while others would stop rifle bullets. They noted that their prices ranged widely.

The administrators were surprised by the many testimonials about the benefits of bulletproof backpacks. They also were surprised that the cost could be less than one hundred dollars. Nonetheless, they made it clear to the parents that the schools would not be purchasing the backpacks.

Some parents changed their minds about bulletproof backpacks when they realized that they would have to pay for them. Others were not deterred. Some reduced the cost by purchasing bulletproof panels that their children could insert into their current backpacks.

RESPONDING TO QUESTIONS ABOUT CHEAP SOLUTIONS

Executives at Nike looked for ways to increase sales of running shoes. They paid billions of dollars to advertising firms. However, they paid nothing to the executives at competing companies to inadvertently promote Nike products.

Educational administrators in Florida looked for ways to better protect students. They paid billions of dollars for security firms to furnish safety devices. However, they paid nothing for anxious parents to furnishe low-cost devices at their own expense.

Attempts to expand shoe sales and school safety were unrelated. Nonetheless, they had some similarities. After you answer the following questions, see if you discern those similarities.

Question 1: Why Did Running Shoe Executives Use High-Priced Marketing?

The executives at Nike wished to ensure that sales of running shoes were strong. They spent billions of dollars getting endorsements and airing ads. They were convinced that these strategies increased sales.

How did different groups respond to the Nike executives? Focus on two groups: the executives at competing firms and consumers.

Did the executives at competing firms have low confidence, moderate confidence, or high confidence in the way that the Nike executives were behaving? How did consumers feel? Explain the bases for your answers.

When answering these questions, as well as those that follow, you can rely on the information in this chapter. You also might rely on some of the sources that are identified in the references at the rear of the book. If you are reading this chapter with colleagues, you are encouraged to converse with them about the best way to answer the questions.

Question 2: Why Did Running Shoe Executives Experiment with No-Cost Marketing?

The executives at Nike never lost confidence in high-priced marketing. Nonetheless, they experimented with no-cost strategies. For example, they prodded competitors into behaviors that promoted the Vaporfly running shoe. They became convinced that these behaviors, which had no costs for Nike, increased sales.

How did different groups respond to the Nike executives? Focus on two groups: executives at competing firms and consumers.

Did executives at competing firms have low confidence, moderate confidence, or high confidence in the way that the Nike executives were behaving? How did consumers feel? Explain the bases for your answers.

Question 3: Why Did Educational Administrators Use High-Priced School Security Devices?

Educational administrators in Florida wished to ensure that students were safe. They spent billions of dollars on facial recognition software and remotely activated door locks. They were convinced that these devices protected students.

How did diverse groups respond to these educational administrators? Focus on two groups: elected officials and parents.

Did elected officials have low confidence, moderate confidence, or high confidence in the way that the educational administrators were behaving? How did the parents feel? Explain the bases for your answers.

Question 4: Why Did Educational Administrators Experiment with No-Cost School Security Devices?

Educational administrators in Florida never lost confidence in high-cost security devices. Nonetheless, they experimented with no-cost-to-school devices. For example, they prodded parents to purchase transparent backpacks or bulletproof backpacks at their own expense. They became convinced that these devices protected students.

How did diverse groups respond to these educational administrators? Focus on two groups: elected officials and parents.

Did elected officials have low confidence, moderate confidence, or high confidence in the way that the educational administrators were behaving? How did the parents feel? Explain the bases for your answers.

SUMMARY

Executives at Nike looked for ways to sell more running shoes. They paid billions of dollars to advertising firms for high-cost marketing. However, they paid nothing when the executives at competing companies inadvertently engaged in pro-Nike behaviors.

Educational administrators in Florida looked for ways to better protect students. They paid billions of dollars to security firms for high-cost safety devices. However, they paid nothing when anxious parents supplied safety devices at their own expense.

Chapter 4

How Effective Are Panic Buttons?

[Portable panic buttons can] send alerts and call for help—instantly!

—Silent Beacon Company, 2021

[Portable panic buttons can] initiate an alert . . . anywhere on the school campus.

—Centegix Company, *2020*

Equipping schools with panic alarms . . . is a commonsense measure.

—New Jersey Governor Phil Murphy, 2019

Each public school [must] implement a mobile panic alert system.

—Florida Senate Bill 70: Alert Systems in Public Schools, 2020

[Portable panic buttons will not be] accidentally pushed . . . [if they are worn] around your neck.

—Kimberline Company, 2020

[Portable] panic buttons . . . can be misplaced or lost.

—Police Chief Tom O'Loughlin, 2014

Education administrators looked for ways to restrain school spending. For example, they substituted low-cost cafeteria meals for more expensive ones.

They also substituted low-cost safety devices for more expensive ones. They contended that substitutions of this sort made budgetary sense and caused no harm.

MONEY-SAVING MEALS

Educational administrators had multiple academic responsibilities. As examples, they had to make sure that students had appropriate textbooks, technology, curricula, and assessments.

The administrators also had nonacademic responsibilities. As examples, they had to make sure that students were safe, comfortable, and fed.

The administrators took all their nonacademic responsibilities seriously. However, they gave special attention to feeding students. They consulted with experts about the best way to prepare lunchroom meals.

Doctors, nutritionists, elected officials, and federal bureaucrats had advice about lunchroom meals. They stated that they should be fresh, balanced, wholesome, and tasty.

The administrators were ready to follow the experts' advice. However, they had to take practical steps before they could prepare meals. They needed to secure recipes, equipment, staff, and food. They also needed to secure the money to implement these steps.

The administrators depended on aid from the federal government. They acknowledged that they would be unable to operate cafeterias without the money and food provided by the National School Lunch Program.

The administrators were able to offer meals at reduced prices because of the federal aid that they received. They offered discounts to all students. They gave heavier discounts to students from low-income households and completely free meals to students from impoverished households.

The administrators depended on the National School Lunch Program. They also depended on their states and school districts. They even depended on local parents, who gave children the money to purchase school meals.

The administrators inevitably encountered students who were supposed to bring lunch money with them but who did not. They cared too much about these children to turn them away unfed. However, they also cared about their budgets.

The administrators did not wish to offer free meals to students who were supposed to pay. They worried that they would take the free meals for granted and expect them indefinitely.

The administrators were genuinely concerned about feeding students and balancing budgets. They believed that they had a way to do both: they would authorize lunchroom charge accounts.

The students who charged meals would be fed. However, they would accumulate debts that their parents would have to settle.

The administrators soon detected a problem with the charge account debts. Some parents were not settling them.

The administrators searched for a solution to the new problem. They soon had one.

The administrators calculated the nutritive values and costs of meals. For example, they compared warm entrees with cold entrees. They concluded that food items from these two groups could have comparable nutritive values but quite different costs. They decided to save money by serving the cold entrees to students with delinquent cafeteria accounts.

Enthusiasts

Educational administrators in more than a dozen states became excited about offering differential cafeteria meals. Those in Warwick, Rhode Island, were especially excited.

The Warwick administrators told parents in their community that they were amending their cafeteria policy. They explained that students who paid off their lunchroom accounts would continue to receive hot and tasty meals. However, students who ran up lunchroom debts would receive a different meal: a slice of American cheese on white bread.

The Rhode Island administrators hoped that those parents who had dutifully been supplying lunch money would support their new plan. They were pleased when some of them replied that they understood the schools' dire financial problems and that they would support differential cafeteria meals.

Skeptics

The Rhode Island educational administrators wondered how parents were responding to their new cafeteria plan. They were pleased that some had expressed confidence. They were nervous when others expressed skepticism.

The skeptical parents recounted how their children had reacted to the cold cheese sandwiches. They reported that they had been so embarrassed that they had tossed the cheese sandwiches uneaten into the trash.

The skeptical parents were upset about the physical effects of skipping meals. However, they were just as upset about the emotional effects. They referred to the new lunchroom policy as "lunch shaming."

The administrators did not want the students to skip lunch. They acknowledged that they may have made an error by offering a substitute sandwich that was not listed on the cafeteria's menu. They were ready to fix this problem by making sure that the substitute sandwich was listed.

The administrators assumed that parents would be mollified by their concession. They were incorrect.

The parents were still irate. They went to journalists. They hoped to recruit them as their allies. They urged them to do an exposé about lunch shaming in the schools. They were excited when the journalists replied with gusto.

Parents across the country learned about the events in Rhode Island. They sympathized with the distraught students and their parents. They wanted to make sure that cafeteria policies of this sort were not replicated in their own states. They went to their elected officials.

A broad coalition of parents asked elected officials to enact state regulations that precluded lunch shaming. They were excited when the officials in more than a dozen states complied with this request.

MONEY-SAVING SAFETY DEVICES

Educational administrators tried to meet regularly with all their constituents. They listened attentively to their concerns and advice. However, they were more attentive to elected officials. They had to be because the officials controlled their funding.

The elected officials were eager to express concerns and give advice. They had strong opinions about teachers, curricula, textbooks, tests, technology, sports, physical facilities, diversity, job training, college prep, libraries, transportation, accreditation, school security, and student safety.

The elected officials served at various levels. They held positions in local, state, or national government. As a result, they had distinct perspectives about the most critical issues for schools.

Although the elected officials frequently had disagreed with each other before 2018, they had a common focus that year. They had been horrified after a former student returned to his Miami-area high school, pulled out weapons, and opened fire on students and staff.

The elected officials were concerned about school safety. Those in Florida displayed the most intense concern. They wished to prevent another event like the one that they had witnessed in Miami.

Florida's officials directed educational administrators to "harden" their schools against dangerous intruders. They had begun to provide them with a "safe schools allocation" in 2017. They promised to increase that allocation.

Florida's educational administrators appreciated the increase in the "safe schools allocation." However, they calculated that it was not adequate to implement the directives that they had been given.

The administrators had been directed to hire armed and trained police officers for every campus. They did not have the money for their salaries.

They therefore decided to hire safety officers who had less training and lower salaries.

The administrators placed advertisements for low-wage safety positions. However, they had a tough time filling the positions. They found out that the persons who would work for those wages could not complete the rigorous training.

The administrators had no choice but to hire highly trained and fully credentialed police officers. They then had to find the money to pay them. They wondered if they then could reallocate some of the money that they had budgeted for school safety devices.

The administrators went to commercial security firms. They told them that they were looking for inexpensive security devices.

The sales teams at these firms immediately sized up the situation. They recommended portable security alarms. They referred to these devices as "panic buttons."

The sales teams noted that portable panic buttons could be components of elaborate safety systems. For example, the buttons could be connected to campus video cameras. If buttons were pressed, they would send a signal to the security firm. The firm would then alert local police officers and connect them to the live video feeds from the endangered schools.

The sales teams would charge millions of dollars to outfit a medium-sized school district with an elaborate safety system. They explained that they had to charge this amount to pay for the panic buttons, auxiliary equipment, maintenance, and monitoring.

Most school administrators judged that the costs were too high for them. They believed that they could reduce them. For example, they could purchase cheaper models of panic buttons, limit the number of persons who carried them, reduce the tech devices to which they were synchronized, and decline the use of auxiliary services.

The school administrators were intrigued by low-cost plans for panic buttons. They believed that they could rely on them without jeopardizing their students. They also believed that they could rely on them without jeopardizing their budgets.

Enthusiasts

Educational administrators were enthusiastic about panic buttons. They wondered whether the elected officials in their states were as enthusiastic.

The educational administrators had been prodded to improve their safety plans after the 2018 tragedy at a Florida high school. They were under enormous pressure from their governors.

The governors examined the school safety plans in their states. They wanted to make sure they were adequate. They also examined the plans in other states. They wanted to see if they had features that they should replicate.

Phil Murphy was governor of New Jersey in 2018. He was heartbroken by the events at the high school in Florida. He announced that he would take steps to prevent similar events in New Jersey.

Murphy examined the tragedy in Florida. He also examined the school safety plan that Florida's governor, Ron DeSantis, had formulated. He noted that DeSantis had pledged to place gun-toting police officers in every school.

Murphy had concerns about the Florida plan. He worried about its expense. He also worried about some of its inadvertent consequences. He concluded that armed police officers could inadvertently harm innocent students, teachers, and staff.

Murphy told his constituents that he would not send the schools more police officers. He preferred to send them panic buttons.

Parents in New Jersey were impressed when their governor characterized panic buttons as extremely cheap, extremely safe, and extremely effective. Parents in many other states were impressed as well. They stated that they would support panic buttons.

Skeptics

Educational administrators had to deal with the elected officials in their state. They noted that officials in New Jersey had come out in favor of panic buttons. They realized that the officials in their respective states could take the same stance.

The elected officials in Florida had not taken the same stance as those in New Jersey. They had come out in favor of armed officers in schools.

The Florida officials were aware that some educational administrators in their state were purchasing panic buttons. They told them that these devices were acceptable. However, they made it clear that they were not obligatory.

The Florida officials later changed their minds. They stated that panic buttons would become obligatory for all schools. They emphasized that armed police officers also would remain obligatory.

The educational administrators had an obvious reason for being interested in the opinions of elected officials. They realized that they determined the amount of money that they received and set restrictions on the way they could spend it.

The educational administrators were also interested in the opinions of parents. They again had an obvious reason: safety plans floundered when parents did not support them.

Many parents had supported the state officials and administrators who had championed panic buttons. However, they later learned that some of these persons had links to lobbyists. They then changed their minds.

The educational administrators realized that they needed more support for panic buttons. They looked for another group to endorse them. They went to police officers. They asked if they approved of the devices.

The police did approve of panic buttons. They predicted that most teachers would use them appropriately. However, they warned that some of them would create problems with them.

The police explained that teachers could unintentionally press panic buttons and trigger false alarms. They added that they also could misplace them. The persons who recovered misplaced panic buttons could trigger them inappropriately.

The police could not predict the number of false or inappropriate alarms that would occur in a district. However, they had learned from experience that some were inevitable. They warned that they could inflict psychological and emotional damage to students.

RESPONDING TO QUESTIONS ABOUT MONEY-SAVING INTERVENTIONS

Educational administrators served warm but expensive meals to students. They expected the students to pay some of the meals' costs. They served cold and inexpensive meals to those who did not pay. Although they admitted that the substitute meals were less tasty, they insisted that they were just as nutritious.

Educational administrators purchased effective but expensive safety devices. However, they were expected to pay some of the costs. They purchased inexpensive panic buttons when they could not pay. Although they admitted that panic buttons were less costly, they insisted that they were just as effective.

Question 1: Why Did Educational Administrators Offer Warm Cafeteria Meals to All Students?

Educational administrators traditionally provided students with warm and nutritious cafeteria meals. They expected most students to pay some of the costs. They allowed those who did not pay to charge their meals. They contended that this practice ensured that all students had satisfying meals.

How did different groups respond to the administrators? Focus on two groups: the students and their parents.

Did the students have low confidence, moderate confidence, or high confidence in the way that the administrators were behaving? How did their parents feel? Explain the bases for your answers.

When answering these questions, as well as those that follow, you can rely on the information in this chapter. You also might rely on some of the sources that are identified in the references at the rear of the book. If you are reading this chapter with colleagues, you are encouraged to converse with them about the best way to answer the questions.

Question 2: Why Did Educational Administrators Offer Cold Cafeteria Meals to Some Students?

Educational administrators urged students to pay off their cafeteria debts. They gave cold, Spartan meals to those who did not pay. They contended that this practice made sense because they could feed indebted students without jeopardizing their budgets.

How did different groups respond to the administrators? Focus on two groups: the students and their parents.

Did the students have low confidence, moderate confidence, or high confidence in the way that the administrators were behaving? How did their parents feel? Explain the bases for your answers.

Question 3: Why Did Educational Administrators Purchase Expensive Safety Devices?

Educational administrators purchased effective but expensive safety devices. They sometimes had to pay with funds from their operating budgets. They contended that this practice ensured that all students were protected.

How did different groups respond to the administrators? Focus on two groups: elected officials and parents.

Did the elected officials have low confidence, moderate confidence, or high confidence in the way that the administrators were behaving? How did parents feel? Explain the bases for your answers.

Question 4: Why Did Educational Administrators Turn to Inexpensive Panic Buttons?

Educational administrators sometimes could not afford expensive safety devices. They then turned to inexpensive panic buttons. They contended that this practice made sense because they could protect all students without jeopardizing their budgets.

How did different groups respond to the administrators? Focus on two groups: elected officials and parents.

Did the elected officials have low confidence, moderate confidence, or high confidence in the way that the administrators were behaving? How did parents feel? Explain the bases for your answers.

SUMMARY

Educational administrators served warm cafeteria meals to students. They expected many of them to pay some of the costs. They substituted cold meals for those who were expected to but did not pay. They insisted that the substituted meals, although less tasty, were still nutritious.

Educational administrators acquired expensive safety devices for their schools. They then were expected to pay for some of the costs. Those who could not pay turned to less costly items, such as panic buttons. They insisted that the panic buttons, although less expensive, were still effective.

Chapter 5

How Effective Are Weapon-Detecting Dogs?

[Weapon-detecting dogs] can screen 150 students per minute.

—Detection Dog Advocate Michael Jacobs, 2018

[Weapon-detecting] dogs act as a great deterrent.

—Sheriff's Officer Ryan Flood, 2019

[Weapon-detecting dogs] are prone to false alerts.

—ACLU Representative Lisa Sullivan, 2011

[Weapon-detecting dogs] disrupt the entire education process.

—Community Agency Director Vinnie Cervantes, 2019

I am suspending . . . dog searches [in my school district because of the problems they create].

—Superintendent Pamela Baldwin, 2019

Elected officials in New York City directed police officers to deal with subway criminals. However, they later reassigned this responsibility to transit workers.

Educational administrators directed police and school resource officers to deal with armed students. However, they later reassigned this responsibility to specially trained dogs and their handlers.

POLICE ON SUBWAYS

Over four million persons work in New York City. Many of them walk, bike, or drive to their jobs. The rest of them rely on public transportation.

New York City's public transportation system is large and complex. It encompasses buses, trains, ferries, and subways. It must accommodate millions of commuters each day.

One-third of the commuters take the subways. They choose them because they are accessible, reasonably priced, and reliable.

Some commuters refuse to take the subways. Although they admit that they would like to use them, they do not because the trains and stations are defaced with graffiti, filled with trash, and infested with rats. Even commuters who used the subways acknowledged these problems.

The commuters reported subway problems to the managers at the New York City Transit Authority. However, they rarely received responses to their complaints.

Although the commuters were concerned about subway filth and disrepair, they were more concerned about subway crime. They routinely witnessed assaults and robberies in the trains and at the stations.

The commuters complained about subway crime to the police. They reported that the criminals were roaming freely on trains and through stations. They pleaded with officers to deal with them.

The police listened attentively to the commuters. They told them that the situation they described was appalling. They agreed with them that subways did not have enough officers to handle the many criminals. However, they could not help.

The police explained that they did not have the funds to hire more officers. They noted that the city officials recently had taken away the funds that they would need. They encouraged distraught commuters to speak to these officials.

The commuters contacted their elected officials. They asked whether they truly had reduced the funds for subway police.

The elected officials admitted that they had reduced these funds. However, they explained that they had reduced them because of allegations that officers had been rude, unprofessional, and racist. They hoped that the commuters would understand the need to punish the police.

The commuters were not understanding. They wished to be safe. They wanted more police on subways.

The elected officials were in a tricky situation. They had reduced the number of subway police to appease commuters. However, they had made it easier for criminals to prey on innocent victims.

The elected officials genuinely did wish to keep commuters safe. They realized that they needed an alternative plan to achieve this goal. They hoped to find one that was economical as well as effective.

The officials had a clever idea. They directed uniformed transit workers to patrol the subway trains and stations. They anticipated that their presence would deter criminals.

The officials had another reason for directing transit workers to patrol the subways. They believed that they would reduce the number of fare beaters—the commuters who rode the subways without purchasing tokens.

The officials had seen online videos in which gangs of teenage fare beaters agilely leapt over the turnstiles at subway entrances. Although they had directed the police to focus on the fare beaters, the officers did not want to divert their attention from more serious offenders.

The officials anticipated that patrolling transit workers would catch more fare beaters than the patrolling police. However, they would earn lower salaries. They were sure that they would generate hundreds of millions of dollars in revenue.

Enthusiasts

The elected officials believed that transit workers would be just as effective as the police at deterring violent criminals. They believed that they would be even more effective at deterring fare beaters. They were eager to see how commuters were responding to this plan.

Two groups of commuters had been disconcerted on the subways. One had been disconcerted by dangerous criminals. The other had been disconcerted by unprofessional police officers.

The group that feared criminals were skeptical of the transit-worker-staffed plan. Nonetheless, they did concede that this plan would be cheap to implement. They had to wait until it was implemented before they had the data to judge whether it was effective at stopping crime.

The group that feared police had been enthusiastic when the elected officials had reduced police patrols. Although they preferred that they appoint no patrols whatsoever, they were willing to settle for transit worker patrols.

The elected officials were interested in one more group: transit workers. They asked the subway managers how their workers felt about confronting violent criminals.

The managers admitted that their workers were worried. They believed that they could allay some of their worries with assurances that police officers would be ready to back them up.

The transit workers were not satisfied with a promise of police backup. They were in a bind because they could not afford to quit their jobs. They therefore went on subway patrols but made little effort to stop criminals or fare beaters.

Skeptics

New York City's journalists reported regularly about subway criminals. They stated that they were out of control

Commuters agreed with the journalists that subway criminals were out of control. Many of them had witnessed assaults or even been assaulted.

Commuters believed that they knew the reason that the subway criminals had become bolder. They were sure that they realized that the subways were now police-free. They wanted the police patrols to return.

The transit workers gave personal reports about subway crime. They had witnessed violent acts but felt unprepared to intervene. They agreed with commuters who wanted the police patrols to return.

The elected officials did not wish to abandon their new safety plan. Nonetheless, they realized that commuters, transit workers, police officers, and journalists were all opposed to it. They had to think carefully about whether to reinstate the police patrols.

DOGS AT SCHOOL

Parents were continually contacting educational administrators about school security. They stressed its importance. They demanded that administrators take precautionary steps to keep children safe.

The educational administrators agreed with the parents. They told them about the steps that they already had taken. As examples, they were using security personnel and electronic surveillance to prevent armed intruders from getting into schools.

The parents supported precautions to deter and detect dangerous intruders. However, they also wanted precautions to deter and detect the dangerous students on the school campuses. They noted that some students were bringing weapons with them to school.

Parents had learned about weapon-bearing students from their own children. They had listened to them recount their terrifying encounters with their armed peers. They had gathered additional information from the media.

The parents discovered that students had complex motives for bringing weapons to school. Some brought them to assault teachers, staff, and peers. Others brought them for self-defense. Still others brought them as a display of bravado.

The parents were sure that weapons did not belong at school. They expected the administrators to locate them, confiscate them, and punish the offenders.

The administrators agreed to ban all weapons. However, they intended to concentrate on knives and guns. They noted that knives were the most common weapons. They added that guns were the deadliest. They fully appreciated the harm that both types of weapons could inflict.

The administrators had police officers and resource officers on duty at their schools. They directed them to search for knives and guns in students' clothing, purses, backpacks, desks, and lockers.

Parents were cautious. They worried that the police and resource officers would be unreasonably intrusive during searches. They also worried that they would be racially biased. They feared that they could cause serious emotional harm to innocent students.

The administrators respected the cautious parents. Nonetheless, they still wanted to locate weapons. They looked for an alternative way to locate them. They asked local law enforcement personnel for suggestions.

The law enforcement personnel had advice. They had been relying on "sniff dogs" to assist them during searches. Although they primarily used them to detect drugs, they sometimes used them to detect guns.

The administrators were excited. They doubted that parents who distrusted police would distrust the sniff dogs. They believed that these dogs might be the ideal solution for their problem. They became even more excited when local law enforcement personnel offered to supply the schools with fully trained sniff dogs.

Some law enforcement personnel conducted dog searches at school for free. Others conducted them for a fee. Still others urged the administrators to hire commercial sniff dog firms to conduct searches for them.

Enthusiasts

The educational administrators had been under pressure to locate and confiscate weapons. They expected the dogs to locate them. They expected their handlers to confiscate them. They assumed that parents would be pleased.

Some parents agreed with the administrators that weapon-detecting dogs would make schools safer. They were pleased.

The administrators were excited by the parents who expressed confidence in weapon-detecting dogs. They hoped that students would have similar confidence.

Some students were optimistic. They believed that the dogs might be able to identify dangerous peers. However, they wanted to see them in action before they made a final decision.

Skeptics

Not all parents had confidence in weapon-detecting dogs. Some were skeptical. The skeptics wished to investigate.

The skeptical parents discovered that the dogs had problems. They found out that they made high numbers of errors when they were searching in busy locations such as airports, bus stations, stadiums, and arenas. They worried that they would make high numbers of errors when they were patrolling school hallways, auditoriums, sports facilities, and playgrounds.

The educational administrators tried to calm the skeptical parents. They insisted that the dogs would have few problems. They offered to experiment with them so that the parents could make up their minds. They were excited when the parents agreed.

After the dogs were introduced in schools, parents asked their children and their children's friends about them. They wanted to know whether the dogs made them feel safer than they had felt with the police and resource officers.

The children responded candidly. They explained that the police and resource officers had frequently failed to detect guns and knives. They noted that the dogs, although they were better than the police at detecting guns, were completely useless at detecting knives. Because knives were the most common weapons at school, they still felt unsafe.

The children had other reasons for objecting to the dogs. Some had a peculiar psychological dread of them, some were allergic to them, and some were upset by the disruption that accompanied them.

The parents listened intently as their children and their friends described their experiences with the dogs. However, they still wanted additional information before they made up their minds.

The parents went to their children's teachers. They asked about their experiences with the dogs. They hoped that the teachers would be as candid as their children and their children's friends had been. They were not disappointed.

The teachers stated that the dogs created turmoil when they patrolled the schools. As a result, they made it impossible to conduct serious academic learning. They doubted that the few weapons that the dogs had found justified the disruption they had caused.

The parents had heard enough. They met with principals, superintendents, and school board members. They pleaded with them to fire the dogs and replace them with police and resource officers.

RESPONDING TO QUESTIONS ABOUT RISKY INTERVENTIONS

Elected officials in New York City listened to numerous complaints about subway crime. They directed police officers to bring crime under control. However, they then had to deal with those residents who distrusted police officers.

The distrustful residents complained that the police officers did not have the appropriate dispositions and skills to handle criminals. They demanded that another group pick up this responsibility. They withdrew their objections after the elected officials reassigned this responsibility to transit workers.

Educational administrators listened to numerous complaints about weapons at school. They directed police and resource officers to locate the weapons, confiscate them, and arrest the perpetrators. However, they then had to deal with those parents who distrusted police and resource officers.

The distrustful parents complained that the police and resource officers did not have the appropriate dispositions and skills to handle armed students. They demanded that another group pick up this responsibility. They withdrew their objections after the administrators reassigned the responsibility to specially trained dogs and their handlers.

The attempts to reduce subway crime and school weapons were unrelated. Nonetheless, they had some similarities. After you answer the following questions, see if you discern those similarities.

Question 1: Why Did Elected Officials Assign Subway Crime to Police Officers?

Elected officials in New York City were concerned about escalating subway crime. Confident that police officers had the dispositions and skills to handle this problem, they told them to get the situation under control.

How did different groups respond to the elected officials? Focus on two groups: commuters and transit workers.

Did commuters have low confidence, moderate confidence, or high confidence in the way that the elected officials were behaving? How did the transit workers feel? Explain the bases for your answers.

When answering these questions, as well as those that follow, you can rely on the information in this chapter. You also might rely on some of the sources that are identified in the references at the rear of the book. If you are reading this chapter with colleagues, you are encouraged to converse with them about the best way to answer the questions.

Question 2: Why Did Elected Officials Reassign Subway Crime to Transit Workers?

The elected officials listened to critics complain that subway police did not have the right dispositions and skills to handle subway criminals. They reassigned this responsibility to transit workers.

How did different groups respond to the elected officials? Focus on two groups: commuters and transit workers.

Did the commuters have low confidence, moderate confidence, or high confidence in the way that the elected officials were behaving? How did the transit workers feel? Explain the bases for your answers.

Question 3: Why Did Educational Administrators Assign Weapon Detection to School Police and Resource Officers?

Educational administrators were concerned about the increasing number of weapons at school. Confident that school police and resource officers had the dispositions and skills to handle this problem, they directed them to locate the weapons, confiscate them, and arrest the perpetrators.

How did diverse groups respond to these educational administrators? Focus on two groups: parents and students.

Did the parents have low confidence, moderate confidence, or high confidence in the way that the educational administrators were behaving? How did the students feel? Explain the bases for your answers.

Question 4: Why Did Educational Administrators Reassign Weapon Detection to Dogs and their Handlers?

Educational administrators listened as critics complained that school police and resource officers did not have the right dispositions and skills to handle students with weapons. They reassigned this responsibility to specially trained dogs and their handlers.

How did diverse groups respond to these educational administrators? Focus on two groups: parents and students.

Did the parents have low confidence, moderate confidence, or high confidence in the way that the educational administrators were behaving? How did the students feel? Explain the bases for your answers.

SUMMARY

Elected officials in New York City were concerned about crime on the subways. They directed police officers to bring the situation under control. After they were badgered by critics of the police, they reassigned this responsibility to transit workers.

Educational administrators were concerned about weapons at school. They directed school police and resource officers to bring the situation under control. After they were badgered by critics of the police and resource officers, they reassigned this responsibility to specially trained dogs and their handlers.

Chapter 6

How Effective Is Therapeutic Yoga?

The positive effects of [yoga] include decreased . . . anger.

—Parent Wuf Shanti, 2017

Yoga may not be the only way to reduce violence, but it can be a start.

—Yoga Instructor Kimaya Singh, 2013

After six weeks of yoga . . . [the school] bullies were bullying less.

—Calming Kids Yoga Founder Dee Marie, 2017

It's time to prevent school violence with meditation.

—Transcendental Meditation Instructor Linda Egenes, 2018

Is the push to teach meditation in schools just a way to mold shiny corporate humanoids?

—Parent Elissa Strauss, 2016

[Yoga contains] religious practices that we don't want our children doing in our schools.

—Parent Susan Jaramillo, 2018

Food industry executives traditionally had used all-meat hamburgers to spur sales. However, they experimented with plant-based burgers. They concluded that both products had benefits.

Educators traditionally had used regulation and punishment to control violent students. However, they experimented with therapeutic yoga. They concluded that both procedures had benefits.

AN UNUSUAL BURGER

Executives in the food industry spent enormous sums marketing all-meat hamburgers. They then carefully monitored how consumers were responding.

Consumers responded enthusiastically. They ate hamburgers with gusto. They purchased them at restaurants, drive-through eateries, food trucks, and hand carts. They prepared them at home with the ground beef they had purchased at grocery stores.

The executives realized that hamburgers were accounting for fifty percent of beef sales. They could not help but be gratified with their success.

The executives were always on the lookout for new products. For example, they discovered that some competitors were offering vegetarian burgers. They had hardly taken notice of these alternative burgers because they were so unlike their meat counterparts and had modest sales. However, this situation would change.

Ethan Brown wished to create plant-based patties that looked like their meat counterparts. He wanted them to also taste like beef. He and his sales team coined an enticing name—Beyond Beef Burgers.

Brown established his first Beyond Beef Burger factory in 2009. He was amazed at the demand for his patties. He was grossing more than thirty million dollars by 2017. He was grossing almost three times that amount a year later.

Ethan Brown was a staunch competitor. He had to contend with the all-beef burgers in grocery stores and restaurants. He also had to contend with another high-profile plant-based product—the Impossible Burger.

Patrick Brown had established the Impossible Burger company in 2011. He was ready to challenge Ethan Brown.

Patrick Brown was convinced that his vegetarian burger had the appearance, texture, and flavor of a meat hamburger. He incorporated his conviction into a marketing slogan: Made from Plants for People Who Love Meat.

Enthusiasts

The manufacturers of plant-based burgers realized that vegetarian consumers were a large enough group to make their ventures extremely profitable. They carefully monitored how they were responding.

Vegetarians had been eating plant-based patties for decades. However, they had complained that the patties were not particularly flavorful. They had tried to solve this problem by heavily salting the patties.

The vegetarians had another complaint about plant-based patties. They disapproved of their carboard-like texture. They had tried to solve this problem by slathering them with condiments and sauces.

The vegetarians eagerly sampled the new generation of plant-based burgers. They had mixed reactions to them.

Some of the vegetarians were disturbed by the uncanny similarity between the new patties and actual beef patties. However, others were extremely happy. They approved of the appearance, texture, and flavor.

The manufacturers also kept their eyes on meat-eating consumers. They realized that some of them wished to sustain a clean environment, eat healthy, and treat animals in an ethical manner. They hoped to persuade these consumers to purchase plant-based burgers.

The meat eaters relished the flavor of traditional hamburgers. Those who had tried the traditional vegetable patties had been disappointed by them. They complained that they did not resemble hamburgers at all. Although they were skeptical of the novel plant-based burgers, they were willing to try them.

The meat eaters were surprised that the new plant-based burgers looked remarkably like meat hamburgers. Nonetheless, they wanted to see if they tasted anything like them. They were shocked by the results. In fact, those who volunteered for blind taste tests could not differentiate the two products.

One meat-eating consumer remarked that the new plant-based burgers had the same hearty flavor as beef hamburgers. Another remarked that they even had the same burnt edges and pink moist centers. They stated that they were eager to order them at restaurants and purchase them at grocery stores.

Skeptics

Meat industry executives had been keeping their eyes on consumers. They wondered whether they were buying the novel plant-based burgers.

The meat industry executives were not particularly perturbed when plant-based burger sales were modest. However, they became worried as they doubled, tripled, and then quadrupled. They decided to act.

The executives tried to discredit plant-based burgers. They claimed that they were not particularly healthy. They noted that they were packed with sodium. They added that they incorporated highly processed ingredients.

The executives stated that the proponents of plant-based burgers had exaggerated the positive environmental impact of their product. In fact, they doubted that the product was good for the environment.

The executives wondered whether their negative campaign was being effective. They therefore monitored gross annual spending on plant-based burgers. They expected this amount to go down. They were miffed when it continued to grow. They were furious when it exceeded a billion dollars annually.

The executives conducted more research. They discovered that many consumers, including those who were omnivores, said that they preferred plant-based burgers over meat burgers. They also learned that even the consumers who preferred meat burgers stated that they were willing to eat plant-based burgers occasionally.

The meat industry executives realized that meat-eating consumers were malleable. They resolved that they would be just as malleable. They would continue to provide them with meat. However, they would provide them with their own brands of plant-based products.

The meat industry executives created a large menu of vegetarian entrees. They marketed meatless hot dogs, sausages, meatballs, chicken-like nuggets, and burgers. However, they concluded that the greatest demand was for meatless burgers. They therefore focused on this product.

The executives commissioned ads for their plant-based burgers. However, they worried that consumers would discern the inconsistency between these ads and the negative campaign that they originally had commissioned. They decided to ignore the earlier campaign and instead point to the delicious flavor, health advantages, and environmental benefits of their own plant-based burgers.

AN UNUSUAL DISCIPLINARY STRATEGY

Educators realized that they had to exercise a certain level of control over students in order to teach them. They traditionally had relied on regulations. They warned students that they would punish them if they violated their regulations.

Educators were especially concerned about controlling violent students. They sometimes punished them with verbal reprimands or after-school detentions. However, they were willing to use more severe punishments, including arrest and prosecution.

The educators hoped that regulations and punishments would prevent violent students from repeating their offences. They also hoped they would dissuade well-behaved students from ever committing violent offences.

Some educators detected a major fault in the regulation-punishment approach. They noted that it failed to alter the attitudes of violent students. They were on the lookout for a different type of strategy.

The skeptical educators turned to art-based behavioral fields such as music therapy, art therapy, drama therapy, and dance therapy. They noted that the professionals in these fields had developed non-confrontational strategies to help students with emotional problems. They wondered whether they could adapt their strategies for violent students.

The educators who experimented with art-based strategies were pleased with their impact on students' attitudes. However, they believed that meditation-based strategies could have an even greater impact.

The educators investigated the meditation-based activities associated with yoga. They read testimonials from persons who had practiced yoga, developed mindfulness, and then gained greater control of their behavior.

The educators had a choice of religious yoga or therapeutic yoga. Anticipating that religious yoga would be too controversial, they chose the therapeutic version.

The educators decided to experiment with therapeutic yoga. They were excited by the results. They concluded that it had fostered positive behavioral attitudes among their students. They detected changed attitudes even among violent students. They wished to substitute it for regulations and punishments.

The educators believed that yoga would affect students' academic achievement as well as their behavior. They therefore wished to make it part of academic curricula. They believed that it could have a place within the health and wellness curricula at elementary schools. They added that it could be appropriate within the physical education curricula at high schools.

Enthusiasts

The educators wondered how persons were responding to therapeutic yoga. They met with the parents of children who had been disciplined for violent behaviors.

These parents felt that their children had been treated too severely. They were especially upset when they were arrested, incarcerated, and expelled. They believed that therapeutic yoga would be a more reasonable way to help them. They were supportive.

The educators were interested in another group. They wanted to hear from the parents of children who had been threatened by violent students.

These parents stated that their children felt unsafe because they were surrounded by violent students who bullied, harassed, threatened, and sometimes harmed them. They worried that eliminating regulations and punishments would encourage the violent students to display even worse behaviors. Nonetheless, they were willing to experimentally supplement the current disciplinary practices with therapeutic yoga.

The parents of the non-violent students had an ulterior reason for introducing yoga into school environments. Some of them had not been able to afford outside-the-school yoga classes. They viewed school-based yoga as a way to give their children the same advantages as the children who came from wealthier families.

Skeptics

The educators kept their eyes on parents. They were gratified when some of them expressed confidence in school-based yoga.

Not all parents supported the at-school yoga. Some of them questioned the motives of the educators. They noted that the educators were under pressure to protect children. They suspected that they had implemented yoga primarily because it was novel and trendy.

Some parents did not support the yoga for a different reason. They noted that it had originated in religious sects in the Middle East and they worried that it still had links to those sects.

The educators responded defensively. They insisted that they were teaching yoga in a secular manner. They explained that they were relying on videos that had been supplied by for-profit companies.

The skeptics were not impressed. They continued to have doubts about yoga's origin and content. Moreover, they doubted that it was an effective way to control school violence.

RESPONDING TO QUESTIONS ABOUT ANOMALIES

Executives in the food industry depended on established products to spark sales. For example, they depended heavily on meat hamburgers. However, they were open to selling new products. Some of them experimented with plant-based burgers.

Educators depended on established disciplinary strategies to control violent students. For example, they depended heavily on regulations that were accompanied by punishments. However, they were open to alternative strategies. Some of them experimented with therapeutic yoga.

The experiments with plant-based burgers in the food industry and therapeutic yoga in the schools were unrelated. Nonetheless, they had some similarities. As you answer the following questions, see if you can discern those similarities.

Question 1: Why Did Food Industry Executives Market All-Meat Hamburgers?

Food industry executives used established products to spark sales. They depended heavily on all-meat hamburgers. They claimed that these burgers had benefits for both consumers and the meat industry.

How did different groups respond to these executives? Focus on two groups: meat-eating consumers and vegetarian consumers.

Did the meat-eating consumers have low confidence, moderate confidence, or high confidence in the way that the executives were behaving? How did the vegetarian consumers feel? Explain the bases for your answers.

When answering these questions, as well as those that follow, you can rely on the information in this chapter. You also might rely on some of the sources that are identified in the references at the rear of the book. If you are reading this chapter with colleagues, you are encouraged to converse with them about the best way to answer the questions.

Question 2: Why Did Food Industry Executives Experiment with Plant-Based Burgers?

Food industry executives worried that they had overlooked products that could spark sales. They experimented with plant-based burgers. They claimed that these burgers had benefits for both consumers and the meat industry.

How did different groups respond to these executives? Focus on two groups: meat-eating consumers and vegetarian consumers.

Did the meat-eating consumers have low confidence, moderate confidence, or high confidence in the way that the executives were behaving? How did the vegetarian consumers feel? Explain the bases for your answers.

Question 3: Why Did Educators Use Regulations and Punishments?

Educators used established disciplinary strategies to control school violence. They depended heavily on regulations accompanied by strict punishments. They claimed that these disciplinary strategies had benefits for both students and educators.

How did diverse groups respond to these educators? Focus on two groups: parents of frequently disciplined students and parents of rarely disciplined students.

Did the parents of frequently disciplined students have low confidence, moderate confidence, or high confidence in the way that the educators were behaving? How did the parents of rarely disciplined students feel? Explain the bases for your answers.

Question 4: Why Did Educators Experiment with Therapeutic Yoga?

Educators worried that they had overlooked strategies for controlling school violence. They experimented with therapeutic yoga. They claimed that this disciplinary strategy had benefits for both students and educators.

How did diverse groups respond to these educators? Focus on two groups: parents of frequently disciplined students and parents of rarely disciplined students.

Did the parents of frequently disciplined students have low confidence, moderate confidence, or high confidence in the way that the educators were behaving? How did the parents of rarely disciplined students feel? Explain the bases for your answers.

SUMMARY

Executives in the food industry sold hamburgers. Nonetheless, they were open to selling alternative products, such as plant-based burgers. They concluded that both products had benefits.

Educators used regulations accompanied by punishments to control school violence. Nonetheless, they were open to alternative disciplinary strategies, such as therapeutic yoga. They concluded that both strategies had benefits.

Chapter 7

How Effective Is Facial Recognition Software?

Facial recognition[software] is . . . improving security . . . at schools.

—Information Technology and Innovation
Vice President Daniel Castro, 2020

Spying on children [with facial recognition software] won't keep them safe.

—Parent Jim Shultz, 2019

Facial recognition [software] is frequently biased and error-prone.

—AI Now Institute Founder Meredith Whittaker, 2020

[Face recognition software leads] to more racial discrimination and racial profiling.

—Springfield, MA, City Councilor Orlando Ramos, 2019

Long-term car loans had a benefit: they enabled consumers to purchase vehicles that they otherwise could not afford. However, they also had inadvertent consequences.

Facial recognition software had a benefit: it alerted educators to threats that they otherwise could not detect. However, it also had inadvertent consequences.

ERROR-PRONE LOANS

Automotive dealers operated in a highly competitive industry. They frequently had to discount car prices to spur sales. Although they made less from these types of transactions, they continued to rely on them.

The dealers needed a way to compensate for the money they lost through discounted transactions. They concluded that they simply had to sell more vehicles. They were distressed when customers showed up at their showrooms, agreed to purchase vehicles, but then did not qualify for loans.

The dealers complained to the personnel at the loan companies. They blamed them for denying loans to customers with limited monthly income. They believed that they had been too severe when making these denials.

The lenders listened to the dealers. They contended that they only turned down loan applicants who could not afford their monthly car payments. However, they had a solution for this problem.

The lending personnel proposed to extend the repayment periods for car loans. They explained that they had been offering three-year loans. They would offer seven-year loans instead. They predicted that these new loans, which would have lower monthly payments, would be approved for persons who had been turned down for a three-year loan.

Enthusiasts

The dealers were excited about the long-term loans. They told their customers about them. They assured them that they would qualify.

Customers who had modest incomes needed new cars to replace ones that had become unreliable. They desperately needed loans. They hoped that they would qualify for the long-term loans. They eagerly applied for them.

Many medium-income customers already had reliable vehicles. Nonetheless, they were envious of neighbors, friends, and relatives who were driving newer models. They viewed long-term loans as an opportunity to keep up with their peers. They enthusiastically applied for them.

High-income customers typically purchased expensive vehicles. They also were eager to keep up with peers. They took out long-term loans so that they could afford vehicles that were more expensive.

The dealers began offering numerous long-term loans. They kept records of their monthly car sales. They detected an increase. They attributed the increase to the availability of long-term loans.

The dealers also calculated their monthly profits from car sales. They did not see an increase. They attributed this problem to their reliance on discounted pricing.

The dealers went back to the lenders. They explained that they needed to continue discounted pricing to lure customers. However, they needed another source of income to make up for the money they were losing because of discounted pricing.

The dealers reminded the lenders that they were responsible for arranging long-term car loans. They asked for a portion of the profits from these lucrative loans. They beamed when the lenders agreed.

The dealers kept records of the profits that they were making from long-term loans. They realized that the amount was enormous. They predicted that it would exceed the profits they were making from auto sales. They were jubilant when this prediction turned out to be correct.

Skeptics

Automobile customers initially were excited by long-term loans. They realized that the loans enabled them to purchase vehicles that they formerly could not. However, they later changed their minds about the loans. They realized that they had inadvertent consequences.

Some of the customers had not comprehended the terms of a seven-year loan. They had been told that a three-year car loan for twenty-five thousand dollars at twenty percent interest would require monthly payments of seven hundred and forty dollars. They had contrasted this amount with the monthly payments of three-hundred and forty-four dollars on a seven-year loan. They had not realized that the second option more than doubled the total interest that they have to would pay.

Disgruntled customers looked for ways to avoid the interest that they were paying on long-term car loans. They assumed that they could pay off the loans early. However, they discovered that their loans contained provisions requiring them to pay the total interest even if they were to repay the loan early.

The disgruntled customers accused the car dealers and lenders of issuing error-prone loans. They howled in protest.

ERROR-PRONE SOFTWARE

Parents were concerned about dangerous school intruders. They reviewed actual cases to learn more about the intruders. They intended to make this information the basis for policies and procedures to keep intruders out of schools.

Parents discovered that some of the intruders had been strangers. They noted that they had entered schools to which they had no personal connections.

Parents also discovered that some of the intruders had entered schools to which they had connections. For example, they found instances of students who had been expelled from school and prohibited from returning but who had returned anyway.

The parents wanted to limit the number of intruders in the schools. They were especially worried that intruders could enter undetected and attack students. They requested strict monitoring of all persons at the schools.

Educational administrators were queried about their procedures for monitoring visitors to their schools. They replied that staffs were responsible for monitoring them. They explained that their staffs included school resource officers, school police officers, teachers, clerical workers, groundskeepers, and custodians.

The administrators told the parents that their current monitoring procedures had a major benefit. They explained that they relied on persons with whom the parents and their children were familiar and in whom they had confidence.

The administrators told parents that the current procedures had another benefit. They explained that they had been inexpensive to implement. As a result, they did not require the diversion of funds from instruction.

Parents acknowledged that the administrators were relying on trusted staff members. They also acknowledged that they were being frugal. However, they still anticipated problems. Parents worried that the schools' staffs might have to intervene with numerous schoolwide disturbances. They questioned whether they would be overextended. They worried that they could be particularly overextended at high school campuses where students had automobiles.

The parents put pressure on the administrators to demonstrate that their monitoring procedures were adequate. They increased pressure after highly publicized school assaults, such as the one at the Marjory Stoneman Douglas High School in Florida. They pointed out that the monitoring personnel at this campus did not detect a dangerous intruder until he began firing his weapons.

The administrators acknowledged that they could do a better job of monitoring. They agreed to devise a more effective approach. However, they needed assistance.

The administrators contacted commercial security consultants. They asked for their advice.

The commercial security consultants were ready with a proposal. They recommended Facial Recognition Software (FRS). They noted that this technology at one time had been used exclusively by the military and government agencies. However, it now was being used by many employers.

The security consultants gave examples of clients from manufacturing, transportation, technology, retailing, and entertainment. They pointed out how they used FRS technology to monitor the movements of nonemployees at worksites. They also noted how they used it to monitor the movements of their own employees. They were confident that school administrators would find similar uses and detect comparable benefits.

Enthusiasts

The educational administrators told the security consultants that they were excited about FRS. They asked them to estimate the cost to outfit their districts with it.

The administrators reviewed the estimates from the security consultants. They were shocked by the expense. They discovered that moderate-sized school districts would have to spend over a million dollars to set up FRS at their schools. Some of them could not afford it. Others worried that their constituents would complain about its high expense.

Some of the administrators had an ingenious plan to fund FRS. They met with their governors and state legislators. They reminded them that they had been pressuring them to improve school security. They then requested that they provide the necessary funding.

The administrators needed governmental funding for FRS. They also needed parental approval. They tried to persuade parents that this technology was as effective as it was expensive.

The administrators stated that FRS was much more effective than human screening. They guaranteed that it could quickly detect unauthorized strangers, expelled students, persons with restraining orders on them, or sex offenders. They noted that it even could detect students to confirm that they had come to school and then remained there.

Some of the parents were enthusiastic. They had doubted that human monitoring was making a difference. They were hopeful that FRS would have a greater impact.

Skeptics

Parents wanted detailed information about the cost for FRS. They asked about the prices for equipment and software.

The administrators acknowledged that equipment was expensive. They gave an example of a New York school district with only seven schools. They reported that this district had to spend over a million dollars for FRS cameras, monitors, and software.

The parents had realized that schools would have to pay for FRS equipment. However, they wanted to know if they would have to pay for additional services.

The administrators stated that schools would have to pay for ongoing FRS technical support. They added that they also would have to pay for secure sites at which to store FRS data.

The administrators worried that the parents would be disconcerted by the total recurring costs associated with the new monitoring system. They tried to allay those concerns.

The administrators anticipated that government-supplied funds would cover at least some of the equipment costs and possibly all of them. However, they conceded that the district would have to pay for staff, consultants, and data storage.

The parents had an additional concern. They had discovered that FRS could mistakenly identify students, faculty, or staff as intruders. They noted that this type of error was a matter of especial concern for members of racial minorities, who had higher chances of being misclassified than non-minority persons.

The parents were upset about the high error rate for minority groups. They blamed the administrators for failing to thoroughly investigate this problem. They refused to support the use of FRS.

The administrators tried to appease the skeptical parents. They pledged to respond cautiously whenever someone was singled out by FRS. However, they were unable to convince these parents. Some still persisted with FRS, in spite of parental objections. Others gave in to the parents and withdrew their support for it.

RESPONDING TO QUESTIONS ABOUT ERROR-PRONE SERVICES

Automotive dealers realized that customers needed loans to make purchases. They initially offered loans that had short terms and low amounts of interest.

The dealers were disappointed when many customers did not qualify for short-term loans because of the high monthly payments. They began to offer them loans that had long terms, modest monthly payments, but higher total interest. They were pleased when customers took out these loans. However, they were chagrinned when they later complained about disturbing unforeseen consequences.

Educational administrators wished to prevent dangerous persons from entering schools. They initially directed their staffs to look out for them.

The administrators were disappointed when their staff failed to detect dangerous intruders. They began to rely on facial recognition software. They were pleased when parents showed interest in the software. However, they were chagrinned when they later complained about disturbing unforeseen consequences.

The attempts to allay concerns about auto loans and school safety software were unrelated. Nonetheless, they had some similarities. After you answer the following questions, see if you discern those similarities.

Question 1: Why Did Automotive Dealers Offer Short-Term Loans?

Automotive dealers knew that customers had difficulty paying for automobiles. They offered them short-term loans. They hoped that the loans would be popular because they entailed a low amount of total interest.

How did different groups respond to the dealers? Focus on two groups: lenders and customers.

Did the lenders have low confidence, moderate confidence, or high confidence in the way that the dealers were behaving? How did customers feel? Explain the bases for your answers.

When answering these questions, as well as those that follow, you can rely on the information in this chapter. You also might rely on some of the sources that are identified in the references at the rear of the book. If you are reading this chapter with colleagues, you are encouraged to converse with them about the best way to answer the questions.

Question 2: Why Did Automotive Dealers Switch to Long-Term Loans?

Automotive dealers were distressed when customers agreed to purchase cars but did not qualify for short-term loans. They switched to long-term loans. They highlighted the fact that these loans had lower monthly payments than the short-term loans. They deemphasized the fact that they had significantly higher amounts of total interest.

How did different groups respond to the dealers? Focus on two groups: lenders and customers.

Did the lenders have low confidence, moderate confidence, or high confidence in the way that the dealers were behaving? How did customers feel? Explain the bases for your answers.

Question 3: Why Did Educational Administrators Rely on their Staffs to Identify Threatening Persons?

Educational administrators knew that parents worried about threats at school. They directed their staffs to be on the lookout for intruders. They hoped that this plan would be popular because it involved staff members in whom the parents had confidence.

How did diverse groups respond to these educational administrators? Focus on two groups: commercial security personnel and parents.

Did the commercial security personnel have low confidence, moderate confidence, or high confidence in the way that the educational administrators were behaving? How did the parents feel? Explain the bases for your answers.

Question 4: Why Did Educational Administrators Switch to Facial Recognition Software?

Educational administrators were distressed when their staffs failed to detect threatening persons. They began to rely on facial recognition software instead. They emphasized the fact that this software was more dependable than human detection. They deemphasized the fact that it was error prone for racial minorities.

How did diverse groups respond to these educational administrators? Focus on two groups: commercial security personnel and parents.

Did the commercial security personnel have low confidence, moderate confidence, or high confidence in the way that the educational administrators were behaving? How did the parents feel? Explain the bases for your answers.

SUMMARY

Auto dealers highlighted the lower monthly payments that customers would be making with long-term loans. They did not highlight the higher total interest they would be paying.

Educators highlighted the fact that facial recognition software was more reliable than human screening. They did not highlight that it was error prone for racial minorities.

Chapter 8

How Effective Is Restorative Justice?

New York City's public schools . . . reported 17,991 [violent] incidents [last year].

—New York State Comptroller Thomas DiNapoli, 2019

[New York City's residents] should be concerned about crime [in their schools] . . . denial is not an option.

—New York Governor Andrew Cuomo, 2020

[New York City schools should use] restorative justice [because it] seeks to promote individual responsibility and participation, repair harm, and build relationships.

—Center for Court Innovation, 2021

[Restorative justice is] making our schools . . . safe.

—NYC Department of Education Spokeswoman Miranda Barbot, 2020

Restorative justice works: I've seen it up close.

—Former New York City Principal Brandon Cardet-Hernandez, 2019

The executives at the College Board had for decades endorsed the objective scoring of higher education entrance exams. However, they became alarmed when clients depicted this technique as biased. They pledged to introduce bias-free scoring.

New York City's Mayor de Blasio realized that his predecessors had for decades endorsed punitive discipline in the schools. However, he became alarmed when constituents depicted it as biased. He pledged to introduce bias-free discipline.

ADAPTED TESTS

The College Board is a large, complex, and influential organization. Although it is a nonprofit organization, it has annual earnings of more than a billion dollars. It derives a good portion of this income from fee-based college entrance exams, such as the Scholastic Assessment Test (SAT).

The administrators at colleges and universities relied heavily on the SAT. They noted that the scores on it were objectively computed. They assumed that they differentiated students who could handle college courses from those who would struggle. They therefore required that all applicants take the test and submit their scores.

Students realized that their SAT scores could determine whether they were admitted to competitive schools, earned scholarships, or qualified for honors courses. They tried to bolster their scores by purchasing study manuals, hiring private tutors, or enrolling in commercial test-prep programs.

Students with high SAT scores approved of the exam. They appreciated the advantage that it gave them over other applicants.

The students with low SAT scores had a different reaction to the exam. They believed it was biased. They contended that it placed them at a disadvantage because it was not sensitive to their distinctive social and economic experiences.

The low-score students had a practical suggestion about how the College Board executives could reduce the bias in their exam. They wanted them to abandon objective scoring. Their parents agreed with them. Many college faculty members also agreed.

The executives at the College Board acknowledged that the SAT posed special challenges for some students. However, they did not wish to eliminate objective scoring. They contended that this change would make the test unreliable and invalid.

The students were annoyed at the College Board. They took their complaints to college administrators. They urged them to quit making admission decisions on the bases of SAT scores.

Several dozen college administrators agreed with the disgruntled students. They announced that they would no longer require that applicants take the SAT exam.

The College Board executives were not flustered after several dozen clients announced that they had become non-SAT schools. However, they did become agitated when that number expanded. They were in shock when the number of schools grew to twelve hundred.

The executives examined the non-SAT schools. They noted that they included for-profit institutions with high acceptance rates. They were not surprised. They explained that it was to their financial advantage to eliminate the SAT because they then could accept even more students.

The executives continued to examine the non-SAT schools. They were surprised after they spotted highly competitive institutions such as the University of California. They had no cavalier argument with which to dismiss their stance on the exam.

The executives were ready to appease their clients. They told them that they would adapt their scoring technique.

The executives explained that they still would compute objective scores—the percentage of correct answers. However, they also would compute adversity scores.

The executives would calculate adversity scores by gathering social and economic information about the test takers. They would look at the test tasker's' neighborhoods, families, and high schools.

The executives intended to examine multiple factors related to neighborhoods. As examples, they would examine crime rates, poverty rates, housing vacancy rates, and home values.

The executives intended to look at multiple factors related to families. They would gather information about household incomes, the education levels of parents, the primary language spoken by parents, and whether households had a single parent or two parents.

The executives would look at multiple factors related to high schools. They would examine the number of students who received free lunches at the test takers' high schools, the opportunities to take Advanced Placement classes at them, and the rigor of the courses at them.

The executives were going to collapse all this information into a numerical score, which could range from one through one hundred. An adversity score of one would indicate that the test taker had had to deal with social, financial, and academic hardships. In contrast, a score of one hundred would indicate that the person had been the recipient of social, financial, and academic privileges. A score of fifty would indicate that a person was right in the middle of this mix.

Enthusiasts

The College Board executives were excited about the proposal to compute adversity scores. They anticipated that it would appease their fiercest critics.

The executives kept an eye on the low-scoring students. They were especially interested in those who had started the anti-SAT fracas. They were relieved after some of them applauded the use of adversity scores.

The executives also kept an eye on college administrators. They hoped that those who still were requiring the SAT would reaffirm their commitment to it. They also were hopeful that those who had turned away from the SAT would change their minds. They were pleased when some administrators did express confidence.

Skeptics

The College Board executives were interested in how the high-scoring students would react to adversity scores. They also were interested in parents, who typically paid the testing fees for the SAT.

Many of the high-scoring students were not pleased with the adversity scores. They realized that the scores would portray them as the recipients of excessive privilege. They pushed back against the new scores. Their parents pushed back as well.

The executives were prepared for nonminority test takers to resist. However, they were surprised when some minority students joined them.

The resisting minority students anticipated that they would receive disadvantageous adversity scores. They explained that their parents were highly educated, earned higher than average salaries, and lived in more affluent neighborhoods.

The resisting minority students gave another reason that they were likely to receive disadvantageous adversity scores. They explained that they had earned scholarships, attended prestigious high schools, mastered rigorous curricula, and enrolled in AP classes. They realized that these factors could contribute to disadvantageous scores.

ADAPTED DISCIPLINE

Educators in New York City faced a daunting challenge. They worked in an enormous school system. They had to educate one-third of the state's students.

The New York City educators faced serious academic problems. They also faced serious disciplinary problems. They had to manage students who committed more violent assaults than the students in all the state's other schools combined.

Parents recognized that many of the challenges in the New York City schools were critical. Nonetheless, they concluded that reducing student violence was the highest priority. They had been disappointed with the way that educators had handled this particular challenge.

The parents had complained about student violence to teachers, principals, school board members, and the city's chancellor of education. Disappointed with their responses, they had gone to Mayor Bill de Blasio.

The parents asked de Blasio to investigate how educators were handling student violence. They were pleased when he agreed to gather information from principals.

The principals reported to the mayor. They stated that they had been using punitive discipline. They explained that they developed behavioral policies and punished students who violated them.

The principals chose punishments that ranged from mild to severe. They said that a mild punishment might entail after-school detention while a severe one could entail expulsion. They typically reserved the severe punishments for violent students.

The parents did not have confidence in the way that the principals were handling violent students. They wanted them to do more. They wanted them to get tougher with them.

Some parents had children who had been frequently disciplined for violence. They did not support the "get tough" rhetoric. They noted that their children lived in neighborhoods with high crime, high unemployment, and high poverty. They believed that they had been profiled as dangerous because of circumstances over which they had no control.

The critical parents claimed that punitive discipline was ineffective as well as biased. They were especially upset when their children were expelled. They noted that they then were left unsupervised, surrounded by delinquent youths, and likely to be lured into greater violence.

The critical parents complained to Mayor Bill de Blasio. They asked him to terminate all punitive discipline. They urged him to consider a different type of discipline, such as that which was being used in Chicago.

Chicago's school leaders had used restorative justice. They had organized discussion circles in which violent students commented on their misbehavior, the reasons for it, and its consequences. They invited victims, uninvolved students, and school staff to also participate. They contended that the discussion circles "restored" healthy social balances in the schools.

Mayor de Blasio listened to the parents who had lost confidence in punitive discipline. He confided that he also had lost confidence in it. He directed all New York City principals to switch to restorative justice.

Enthusiasts

The mayor had to depend on principals to implement restorative justice. He hoped that they would be supportive. He was pleased when many of them did express support.

The mayor also had to depend on teachers. He hoped that they would be supportive.

Many of the teachers were excited about restorative justice. They were joined by like-minded counselors, social workers, and staff members. They believed that restorative justice would lead to fewer violent students in their schools.

The parents of frequently disruptive students had complained that their children were being unfairly profiled as troublemakers. They had been particularly upset when their children were expelled. They anticipated that restorative justice would keep them at school, supervised, and away from bad social influences. They were supportive.

Skeptics

New York City principals were a progressive-minded group. They had discerned the limitations of punitive discipline. They considered restorative justice to be a promising alternative. They were open to change. Nonetheless, some of them were cautious.

The cautious principals frequently had to deal with violent students. They had the discretion to suspend these students when they brought weapons to school, threatened teachers, assaulted peers, or openly confronted police officers. They wished to retain that discretion.

The mayor assured the cautious principals that they could continue to suspend violent students. However, he required that they first obtain approval from the city's Department of Education.

The principals objected. They explained that they had to respond to dangerous situations immediately. They did not have time for a delayed approval process.

The principals went to the leaders of their professional association and asked them to protest the delayed approval process. They asked local journalists to stir up resistance as well. They were pleased when both groups responded with gusto.

RESPONDING TO QUESTIONS ABOUT ADAPTED INTERVENTIONS

The executives at the College Board had endorsed objective scoring of college entrance exams for decades. They fretted when clients complained that this technique was biased. They pledged to introduce bias-free scoring. They hoped that their clients would approve.

Mayor Bill de Blasio knew that New York City's mayors had endorsed punitive school discipline for decades. However, he fretted when constituents complained that this technique was biased. He pledged to introduce bias-free discipline. He hoped that his constituents would approve.

Question 1: Why Did College Board Executives Endorse Objective Scores?

The executives at the College Board had for decades endorsed objective scores on college entrance exams. They contended that these scores accurately depicted the academic abilities of applicants.

How did different groups respond to the executives? Focus on two groups: college applicants and college administrators.

Did college applicants have low confidence, moderate confidence, or high confidence in the way that the executives were behaving? How did the college administrators feel? Explain the bases for your answers.

When answering these questions, as well as those that follow, you can rely on the information in this chapter. You also might rely on some of the sources that are identified in the references at the rear of the book. If you are reading this chapter with colleagues, you are encouraged to converse with them about the best way to answer the questions.

Question 2: Why Did College Board Executives Endorse Student Adversity Scores?

The executives at the College Board fretted when clients criticized objective scores as biased. They agreed to calculate student adversity scores for their exams. They guaranteed that the adversity scores would be bias-free.

How did different groups respond to the executives? Focus on two groups: college applicants and college administrators.

Did college applicants have low confidence, moderate confidence, or high confidence in the way that the executives were behaving? How did the college administrators feel? Explain the bases for your answers.

Question 3: Why Did New York City's Mayor Endorse Punitive Discipline?

New York City's mayors had endorsed punitive school discipline for decades. They had contended that it reduced the risks from violent students.

How did diverse groups respond to these mayors? Focus on two groups: principals and parents.

Did the principals have low confidence, moderate confidence, or high confidence in the way that the mayors were behaving? How did the parents feel? Explain the bases for your answers.

Question 4: Why Did a New York City's Mayor Endorse Restorative Justice?

Mayor Bill de Blasio was upset when constituents criticized punitive discipline as biased. He endorsed restorative justice instead. He guaranteed that restorative justice would be bias-free.

How did diverse groups respond to this mayor? Focus on two groups: principals and parents.

Did the principals have low confidence, moderate confidence, or high confidence in the way that this mayor was behaving? How did the parents feel? Explain the bases for your answers.

SUMMARY

The executives at the College Board had endorsed objective scoring of college entrance exams for decades. They fretted when clients claimed that this scoring technique was biased. They assured them that they would introduce a bias-free scoring procedure.

Mayor de Blasio was aware that New York City's mayors had supported punitive discipline in schools. However, he fretted when constituents claimed this discipline was biased. He assured them that he would introduce bias-free discipline.

Chapter 9

How Effective Are Cyberbully Laws?

[Everyone should] learn what cyberbullying is.

—American Psychological Association, 2021

Some states consider . . . cyberbullying criminal.

—U.S. Department of Health and Human Services, 2021b

[You can commit a cyberbullying crime in this state by means of] telephone, wireless telephone, or other wireless communication device, computer, or pager.

—Missouri State Statute §160.775, 2016

[Florida's cyberbully] laws cover off-campus conduct [that] substantially interferes with . . . school.

—U.S. Department of Health and Human Services, 2021a

[California's cyberbully law requires that every school] adopt a strong [policy] that specifically [addresses] sexual orientation and gender identity.

—Southern California American Civil Liberties Union, 2021

Criminalizing [cyberbullying] is really not . . . effective.

—Child Trend Advisor Deborah Temkin, 2019

Hospitality officials worried that tourists might avoid Florida because of lightning strikes and shark attacks. They promised to protect them through early detection and warnings.

Elected officials worried that parents might keep their children from school because of cyberbullying and face-to-face bullying. They promised to protect them with special anti-bullying laws.

AVAILABILITY BIAS AFFECTS TOURISTS

State hospitality officials had complex responsibilities. They had to make tourists aware of the sporting venues, recreational facilities, lodgings, restaurants, and theme parks in their states. They then had to persuade them to visit those attractopms.

The hospitality officials realized that governors and legislators had provided the funding for their positions. They anticipated that they would hold them accountable for achieving their goals. They expected them to review reports about the number of tourists that the hospitality officials had attracted each year.

Some hospitality officials found it easy to attract large crowds of tourists. For example, those in Florida attracted more than a hundred million persons annually.

The officials in Florida kept lists of the activities in which the tourists showed the greatest interest. They noted that many of them came to play golf. They therefore highlighted the state's numerous top-tier courses.

The officials noted that many tourists came to Florida to swim. They therefore highlighted their state's gorgeous beaches and year-round temperate climate.

Florida's hospitality officials frowned on problematic destinations. They kept records of poorly maintained parks, blighted beaches, and rundown lodges. Although they were distressed by these problems, they felt relieved that they had manageable solutions.

The officials noted that some problems did not have easy-to-manage solutions. For example, they were aware of the thousands of cloud-to-ground lightning bolts that struck Florida each day. They knew that golfers, who had christened their state the Lightning Capital of America, were aware of the danger that these bolts posed.

The officials tried to reassure the golfers that they were safe. They explained that they were protected by early detection devices and early warning devices on Florida's courses.

The golf course managers had installed the early detection devices. They used them to detect lightning before it posed a danger. They then sounded early warning alarms. They bragged that the early detection and early warning devices had dramatically reduced the number of golfers that were being struck by lightning.

The officials were pleased with the way they had dealt with lightning strikes. However, they had another problem—shark attacks.

The officials had learned from surveys that tourists had a greater fear of sharks than of lightning. They were surprised by these findings because the chance of being harmed by sharks was low.

The officials believed that they had a straightforward way to handle fear of sharks. They publicized data about the low probability of shark attacks. They assumed that these data would calm tourists. However, they discovered that their assumption was incorrect: the tourists were as frightened as ever. They therefore consulted with psychologists.

The psychologists had an explanation for the widespread fear of sharks. They attributed it to availability bias. They explained that availability bias caused persons to worry about some threats but ignore others. They used experiments to illustrate the point.

The psychologists described three groups. One group comprised people who had recently witnessed violent traffic incidents, another group had people who had witnessed loss-of-footing incidents, and the last group had people who had witnessed choking incidents.

Each group had been asked to identify the leading cause of accidental deaths. Based on their experiences, the first group rated car crashes as the leading cause. For similar reasons, the second group rated falls as the leading cause and the third group selected throat obstructions.

The psychologists explained that the experimental groups were affected by incidents that were fresh in their minds. They opined that the tourists were affected by shark attacks because sensational media coverage kept them fresh in their minds.

The hospitality officials wished to reassure frightened tourists. They told them that they were protected by early detection systems and early alert systems at beaches. They explained that Florida lifeguards were on the alert for sharks and would blow their whistles when they detected them.

Enthusiasts

The Florida tourist officials were excited about the safety measures they had implemented. They were eager to see how people would respond to them.

The officials kept their eye on local government leaders. They realized that they were concerned about tourists. They hoped they would pressure businesspeople to implement the new safety measures at golf courses and beaches.

Local government leaders agreed that tourists needed to feel safe. They investigated the costs for early lightning detection and early warning devices. They also investigated the costs for training lifeguards to detect sharks and warn swimmers about them. They were pleased that all these measures were cheap. They quickly purchased equipment and arranged for training.

The Florida tourist officials anticipated that business leaders also would be supportive of safety measures. They were correct.

The business leaders knew that tourists were attracted to Florida's golf courses and beaches. They were eager to convince them that they would be safe at both locations. They were pleased when the tourists continued to visit in droves.

Skeptics

Many tourists were reassured by the safety measures at Florida's golf courses and beaches. However, others remained skeptical.

The skeptics believed that they still were in danger. They warned that the safety measures created merely an illusion of safety. They used social media sites and tourist blogs to air this warning.

AVAILABILITY BIAS AFFECTS PARENTS

Parents set ambitious goals for school superintendents. They expected them to hire qualified teachers, maintain comfortable learning environments, select challenging curricula, and install current technology. They also expected them to keep children safe.

The parents told the superintendents that all their responsibilities were important. Nonetheless, they made it clear that safety was their most important responsibility. They asked them to report regularly about the steps they were taking to keep children safe.

The superintendents were willing to report to the parents. They reported that they had taken steps to deal with dangerous assailants from outside the schools. They had been relying on sophisticated technology and trained personnel. They explained that they used the technology to spot intruders. They authorized the trained personnel to stop the intruders before they caused harm.

The superintendents also had to deal with dangerous assailants from inside as well as outside the schools. They realized that most of the inside assailants were students. They therefore had trained their staffs to identify dangerous students. They expected their staff to intervene before these dangerous students could cause harm.

The superintendents admitted that they had done better with deterring dangerous outsiders than they had with dangerous insiders. They admitted that many dangerous students still roamed their campuses. They were willing to meet with the persons who dealt with dangerous students and get advice about additional steps they should take.

Principals, district disciplinary officers, teachers, and police officers dealt regularly with dangerous students. They all had advice for the superintendents. They told them that schools needed to detect dangerous students before they caused harm. They suggested that they focus their efforts on school bullies.

Parents agreed with this advice. They believed that bullies had taken control of the schools. Many of them had listened to firsthand reports from their children about the bullies who had frightened, humiliated, or harmed them or their classmates.

The superintendents responded that they were quite aware of bullies. They added that they had been trying to deal with them for a long time. They implored the parents to be patient.

The parents were not patient. They were exasperated by futile attempts to stop bullies. They went to their elected state officials to complain.

The state officials sympathized with the parents. They did not want them to wait for their superintendents to produce a plan for dealing with school bullies. They told them that they had their own plan. They would prosecute bullies as criminals.

The officials already had the laws that they would need to prosecute bullies. Nonetheless, they wished to enact new ones They believed that they needed the new laws to handle cyberbullies.

Elected officials in California passed a law to deter cyberbullies. They stated that it would make it easier to prosecute those who were taunting minority students, especially those who were picking on LGBT youths.

Elected officials in Missouri also passed a law to deter cyberbullies. Within it, they listed the devices that the cyberbullies used to torment their victims. They identified these as computers, smart phones, landline telephones, and pagers.

Elected officials in Florida passed a law that focused on the locations from which cyberbullies launched digital assaults. They wished to take care of those who attacked from schools as well as those who attacked from off-campus sites.

The elected officials hoped that parents would be satisfied with their new cyberbullying laws. They were surprised when parents demanded equally explicit laws to cover face-to-face bullying. The officials promised to enact laws for both types of bullying.

Enthusiasts

Elected officials concluded that the superintendents had been unable to control the bullies in their schools. They believed that they had been too restrained. They took matters into their own hands.

The officials wished to ensure that bullies would be punished. They enacted laws to make it easier for the courts to impose these punishments. They were eager to see how parents reacted.

Some parents were enthusiastic. They were hopeful that court-administered punishments would be more effective than school-administered punishments. They hoped that new laws would restrain bullies and protect victims. They indicated that they were supportive of them.

Skeptics

Some parents were satisfied with laws that criminalized bullying. Others were not. The dissatisfied parents believed that these laws might reduce overt acts of aggression by bullies but that they would not change the bullies' attitudes or dispositions.

The parents of children who had been charged with bullying were especially skeptical of the anti-bullying laws. They feared that they would transform their children into hardened criminals. They preferred that their children be sent to caring counselors and sensitive educators rather than hostile police and strict judges.

The officials who had enacted the bullying laws kept their eyes on parents. They also kept them on students. They asked them if bullies at their schools were deterred by the new laws.

The students answered candidly. Some did feel that the bullies were deterred by the new laws. However, most of them doubted that the bullies were even aware of those laws.

RESPONDING TO QUESTIONS ABOUT AVAILABILITY BIAS

Florida's hospitality officials knew that tourists worried about lightning strikes and shark attacks. They hoped that early detection and early warnings would ease their fears.

Elected state officials knew that parents worried about cyberbullying and face-to-face bullying in schools. They hoped that special anti-bullying laws would ease their fears.

The efforts to allay the fears of tourists and parents were unrelated. Nonetheless, they had some similarities. After you answer the following questions, see if you discern those similarities.

Question 1: How Did Florida's Hospitality Officials Deal with Lightning Strikes?

Florida's hospitality officials were concerned about the lightning strikes at golf courses. They announced that they would use early detection devices and early warning devices to protect golfers.

How did different groups respond to the hospitality officials? Focus on two groups: businesspeople and tourists.

Did the businesspeople have low confidence, moderate confidence, or high confidence in the way that the hospitality officials were behaving? How did the tourists feel? Explain the bases for your answers.

When answering these questions, as well as those that follow, you can rely on the information in this chapter. You also might rely on some of the sources that are identified in the references at the rear of the book. If you are reading this chapter with colleagues, you are encouraged to converse with them about the best way to answer the questions.

Question 2: How Did Florida's Hospitality Officials Deal with Shark Attacks?

Florida's hospitality officials were concerned about shark attacks. They announced that they would use lifeguard detection and lifeguard alerts to protect swimmers.

How did different groups respond to the hospitality officials? Focus on two groups: businesspeople and tourists.

Did the businesspeople have low confidence, moderate confidence, or high confidence in the way that the hospitality officials were behaving? How did the tourists feel? Explain the bases for your answers.

Question 3: How Did Elected State Officials Deal with Face-to-Face Bullying?

Elected state officials were concerned about face-to-face bullying at school. They announced that they would enact special anti-bullying laws to protect students.

How did different groups respond to the elected state officials? Focus on two groups: parents and students.

Did the parents have low confidence, moderate confidence, or high confidence in the way that the elected state officials were behaving? How did the students feel? Explain the bases for your answers.

Question 4: How Did Elected State Officials Deal with Cyberbullying?

Elected state officials were concerned about cyberbullying at school. They announced that they would enact special anti-cyberbullying laws to protect students.

How did different groups respond to the elected state officials? Focus on two groups: parents and students.

Did the parents have low confidence, moderate confidence, or high confidence in the way that the elected state officials were behaving? How did the students feel? Explain the bases for your answers.

SUMMARY

The hospitality officials in Florida were concerned about the threats to tourists from lightning and sharks. They used early detection and early warnings to protect them.

The elected officials in many states were concerned about the threats to students from cyberbullying and face-to-face bullying. They used anti-bullying laws to protect them.

Chapter 10

How Effective Are Involuntary Psychiatric Screenings?

[Florida's Baker Act authorizes the] involuntary [psychiatric] examination of a student.

—School District of Lee County, 2021

In Florida, approximately 36,000 kids are Baker Acted per year.

—Journalist Lynn Hatter, 2020

If you have any kind of outburst [in a Florida school] . . . they will Baker Act you.

—Parent Hilary Caskey, 2019

[Some persons who are Baker Acted] are not mentally ill or dangerous.

—Hospital Employee Terry Weaver, 2021

The Baker Act . . . should not be used as a substitute for behavior management.

—Weaver Policy Center Vice-Presidents Vicky Basra & Vanessa Patino-Lydia, 2020

The Baker Act . . . . is not helping [students by] . . . . locking them away.

—Parent Martina Falk, 2020

Librarians were distressed when patrons disregarded lending policies. They believed that strict fines would change their behavior. They were surprised by the actual consequences.

School administrators were distressed when students disregarded disciplinary policies. They believed that involuntary psychiatric detentions and screenings would change their behavior. They were surprised by the actual consequences.

STRICT LIBRARY FINES

Librarians cared about their patrons. They selected interesting and useful books, films, music, and digital resources for them. They then made them available at no cost.

The librarians allowed patrons to use materials at their facilities. They also permitted them to borrow them, remove them from library facilities, and use them at their homes.

The librarians regulated the amount of time for which patrons could borrow materials. Anticipating that some patrons would not adhere to the regulations, they imposed fines. They withdrew patrons' borrowing privileges when they did not pay their fines.

The librarians had confidence in their borrowing regulations. They wondered whether their patrons shared their confidence.

Enthusiasts

Some patrons supported the librarians' borrowing regulations. They agreed that the librarians should impose penalties on patrons who damaged items, returned them late, or did not return them at all.

Some of the supportive patrons had never been fined. Others had been fined rarely. Both groups considered the penalties to be straightforward and fair.

The supporters believed that the fines were needed to change the behaviors of derelict patrons. They also believed that they were needed to create small pools of discretionary money. They expected the librarians to use this money to replace items that had been damaged or that had never been returned.

Skeptics

Frequently fined patrons were skeptical of the borrowing regulations. They readily admitted that they had returned books late or damaged. However, they cited extenuating circumstances.

The patrons with multiple fines explained why they had not complied with borrowing regulations. They blamed inclement weather, unreliable public transportation, dangerous neighborhoods, or homelessness.

Some patrons could not pay their fines. They contended that their incomes were too meager. They urged the librarians to eliminate the fines.

The patrons who had unpaid fines had lost their borrowing privileges. They stated that they still had to depend on the public libraries for books and digital resources. They pleaded with the librarians to reinstate their borrowing privileges.

Some librarians sympathized with the penalized patrons. They believed that the fines were impediments that kept low-income groups away from libraries. They called for a new era of penalty-free libraries.

STRICT PSYCHIATRIC DETENTIONS

Maxine Baker was a twentieth-century state representative in Florida. She began her first term in 1963, quickly secured an appointment to the House Committee on Mental Health, and eventually became its chair.

Baker had access to statistics about the number of Floridians with mental health problems. She was not surprised that the number of adults with mental health problems was high. However, she was staggered that the number of children with these problems was also high.

Baker wished to help the children who had mental health problems. She looked for a group of professionals who had access to these children and who could initiate referrals for assessment and treatment. She believed that teachers would be ideal. She was convinced that they had the training, sensitivity, and opportunities to identify needy children.

Baker discovered that the teachers already had the authority to single out children who might have mental health problems. She asked them why they rarely had used that authority.

The teachers replied that they would have to deal with a complex web of legal and medical constraints. They did not have the time or stamina to navigate the referral process.

Baker promised to change the referral process. She incorporated those changes into a 1971 legislative bill.

Baker's fellow legislators supported her. They believed that her bill would be extremely helpful.

The legislators eponymously referred to the new mental health bill as the Baker Act. They eagerly voted for it. They beamed when the governor signed it. They hoped that their constituents would be pleased.

Constituents were pleased. They realized that their legislators had made it easy to detain persons with possible mental health problems, arrange for psychological screenings, and specify treatments.

Even though they were pleased, constituents wished that the legislators had consulted them before they had finalized the Baker Act. They believed that they could have improved it.

The constituents wanted to expand the group of persons who could trigger involuntary psychiatric detentions and screenings. They wished to include doctors, mental health professionals, judges, and police officers.

The constituents also wanted some restrictions on involuntary detentions. They believed that the detentions should be used only for individuals who were displaying unusual psychiatric behaviors, likely to harm themselves, likely to hurt others, or becoming "self-neglectful." They also believed that they should not last longer than seventy-two hours.

The Florida legislators listened to their constituents. They incorporated their suggestions into an amended version of the Baker Act.

Enthusiasts

Maxine Baker was a politically progressive legislator. When she drafted her mental health bill, she hoped to have the support of likeminded politicians.

Politically progressive legislators stood firmly with Baker. They were distressed that many students with mental health problems had not been diagnosed. They believed that Baker's bill would benefit these students.

Politically conservative legislators also supported Baker. They had been concerned about students who had mental health problems and who were a danger to others at school. They believed that Baker's legislation would benefit students with mental health problems and their potential victims.

The legislators wondered how parents were reacting to their efforts. They realized that they needed the support of parents for the Baker Act to succeed.

The parents had been reading, listening to, and viewing reports about violence at school. They had pored over statistics about the increased frequency and escalating severity of student-on-student attacks.

The parents had concluded that psychologically aberrant youths had been responsible for many of the most violent school attacks. They believed that these youths could have been stopped had they been referred for psychiatric screening and treatment. They supported the Baker Act.

Skeptics

Parents were concerned that their children would be targeted by violent students. They discussed and analyzed the Baker Act while it was being debated in the legislature. They continued to discuss and analyze it after it was implemented in the schools.

Many of the parents had children who had never behaved erratically or violently. They had no reason to believe that their children would ever be detained for involuntary psychiatric screening. They therefore considered the Baker Act to be an appropriate way to reduce the threats from violent students. They had confidence in the Baker Act.

Not all parents had confidence in the Baker Act. Some were skeptical of it. Some of the skeptics had children who had behaved erratically and then been sent away for psychiatric detention and screening. They insisted that their children, even though they had behaved erratically, had never had serious mental health problems.

The skeptical parents feared that the Baker Act was being abused. However, they needed assistance to prove their case. They went to journalists for help.

The journalists were eager to assist. Nonetheless, they explained that they would have to wait to acquire the data they needed. In fact, they had to wait several years before they had sufficient data.

The journalists combed through the details about involuntary detentions. They discovered that the Baker Act had been used to detain more than thirty thousand youths each year. They found examples of youths who clearly had not had mental health problems, who had still been detained, and who had suffered greatly.

The skeptical journalists were particularly interested in young students who had been detained involuntarily. They reported extensively about a six-year-old girl who had been placed in handcuffs and sent away without parental consent. They claimed that this innocent girl typified many of the other young children who had been "Baker Acted."

RESPONDING TO QUESTIONS ABOUT STRICT INTERVENTIONS

Librarians fined patrons who borrowed books but did not return them on schedule. They suspended their borrowing privileges if they did not pay the fines. They were surprised at the impact that this policy had on patrons from low-income neighborhoods.

Florida's educational administrators were concerned about students who might have mental health problems and who might be dangerous. They used the Baker Act to arrange 72-hour nonconsensual psychiatric detentions and screenings. They were surprised at the impact that the Baker Act had on students who never had exhibited symptoms of mental health problems and who never had shown signs of being dangerous.

The actions of the librarians and the educational administrators were unrelated. Nonetheless, they had some similarities. After you answer the following questions, see if you discern those similarities.

Question 1: Why Did Librarians Revoke Borrowing Privileges?

Librarians fined patrons who did not return books on schedule. They then revoked the borrowing privileges of those who did not pay the fines. They reasoned that these strict interventions were necessary to change the patrons' behaviors and prevent them from disrupting library operations.

How did different groups respond to the librarians? Focus on two groups: patrons who were fined frequently and those who were fined rarely.

Did the patrons who were fined frequently have low confidence, moderate confidence, or high confidence in the way that the librarians were behaving? How did the patrons who were rarely fined feel? Explain the bases for your answers.

When answering these questions, as well as those that follow, you can rely on the information in this chapter. You also might rely on some of the sources that are identified in the references at the rear of the book. If you are reading this chapter with colleagues, you are encouraged to converse with them about the best way to answer the questions.

Question 2: Why Did Some Librarians Refuse to Revoke Borrowing Privileges?

Some librarians refused to revoke borrowing privileges. They reasoned that too many patrons from low-income neighborhoods would suffer inordinately from this intervention.

How did different groups respond to the librarians? Focus on two groups: patrons who were fined frequently and those who were fined rarely.

Did the patrons who were fined frequently have low confidence, moderate confidence, or high confidence in the way that the librarians were behaving? How did the patrons who were rarely fined feel? Explain the bases for your answers.

Question 3: Why Did Florida's Educational Administrators Arrange Involuntary Psychiatric Detentions and Screenings?

Florida's educational administrators were concerned about students who might have mental health problems and who might be dangerous. They relied on the Baker Act to arrange 72-hour involuntary psychiatric detentions and screenings. They reasoned that the detentions and screenings were necessary to prevent these students from harming themselves or others.

How did different groups respond to these educational administrators? Focus on two groups: parents of students who had been detained and parents of students who had never been detained.

Did the parents of students who had been detained have low confidence, moderate confidence, or high confidence in the way that these educational administrators were behaving? How did the parents whose children had never been detained feel? Explain the bases for your answers.

Question 4: Why Did Some Florida Educational Administrators Refuse to Arrange Involuntary Psychiatric Detentions and Screenings?

Some educational administrators refused to arrange involuntary psychiatric detentions and screenings. They reasoned that too many innocent students would suffer from these procedures.

How did different groups respond to these educational administrators? Focus on two groups: parents of students who had been detained and parents of students who had never been detained.

Did the parents of students who had been detained have low confidence, moderate confidence, or high confidence in the way that these educational administrators were behaving? How did the parents whose children had never been detained feel? Explain the bases for your answers.

SUMMARY

Librarians tried to change the behaviors of patrons who did not return books on schedule. They fined them. They then revoked their borrowing privileges if they did not pay their fines. Florida's educational administrators tried to change the behaviors of students who appeared to be dangerous. They sent them for nonvoluntary psychiatric detentions and screenings. Both groups had to deal with critics who were alarmed about the inadvertent consequences of these penalties.

Chapter 11

How Effective Are Gun-Carrying Teachers?

It will surprise no one if Florida finds itself with a new [school massacre like the one at] Parkland.

—*Palm Beach Post* Editorial Board, 2021

In Florida, teachers can carry guns at school.

—Journalist Katie Mettler, 2019

I'm very thankful [I can carry a gun].

—Florida Teacher Steve Stokes, 2019

The exact number of Florida teachers with guns remains under wraps.

—Journalist Ana Ceballos, 2019

Not having that number [of gun-carrying teachers] is not a bad thing.

—Florida State Senator Manny Diaz, 2019

Arming teachers in the state of Florida is not a real solution [for school assaults].

—Florida Education Association President Fedrick Ingram, 2019

Florida's legislators authorized bonuses for teachers with high test scores. They were then challenged to reveal the number of minority-group teachers who were recipients.

Florida's legislators authorized teachers to carry guns at school. They were then challenged to reveal the number of teachers who were carrying them.

BONUS-WINNING TEACHERS

Florida legislators wished to start a lottery during the 1990s. They viewed it as a prime opportunity to raise state revenue.

The legislators had to get voters to approve a lottery. They knew that they would have questions about it. They tried to anticipate them. For example, they were sure that they would want to know how lottery revenue would be used.

The legislators were prepared for this question. They answered that the lottery revenue would be reserved for students. They explained that it would pay for scholarships awarded to extremely bright students.

The legislators explained that too many bright high school graduates left Florida to attend universities in other states. They noted that they then formed friends, met spouses, accepted jobs, and became residents of those states.

The legislators wanted to halt the migration of bright students. They had a plan to keep them at home. They would give them full-tuition scholarships that they could use at any Florida university.

The legislators realized that the scholarships would be pricey. They therefore intended to offer them only to students with truly superior academic aptitude. They would require that these students meet several criteria. For example, they would require them to achieve a high score on a college entrance exam.

Floridians were intrigued by their legislators' plan. They were delighted that they could fund it completely from lottery money. They told them to get started.

The legislators were excited that they had voter approval. They soon had implemented the lottery and begun to make awards. They referred to the awards with a catchy name: Bright Futures Scholarships.

Twenty years later, the legislators still recalled the public excitement that the Bright Futures Scholarships had engendered. In fact, they searched for an educational proposal that would recreate that excitement.

The legislators devised another scheme that centered around scholarships. This time, they focused on teacher scholarships. They explained that extremely bright teachers were being lured to other states by jobs with higher salaries. They wished to keep these teachers in Florida.

The legislators had a plan. They would pay cash bonuses to superior teachers. They would require that teachers demonstrate their superiority by several criteria, the key one of which was a high score on a college entrance exam. They referred to their plan as Best and Brightest Teacher Scholarship Program.

Enthusiasts

The legislators had focused their scholarship program on teachers. They kept their eyes on the teachers to see how they were reacting.

The teachers were concerned about test scores that they had earned when they had entered college. They went back and examined them. Those with the high scores realized that they would qualify for scholarships. Many of these high-scoring teachers supported the program.

The legislators also were interested in how parents were reacting to the teacher scholarships. They had hoped that they would exhibit the same enthusiasm that they had displayed for student scholarships.

The parents noted that the new scholarships were reserved for teachers of exceptional academic aptitude. They wanted these teachers in their children's classrooms. They judged that a test score was a valid measure of academic aptitude. They therefore supported the scholarship plan.

Skeptics

Not all teachers supported the scholarship program. Veteran teachers were particularly skeptical of it.

The veteran teachers had completed college entrance exams decades earlier. They feared that their scores would be significantly lower than the teachers who had taken the exams more recently. They were not enthusiastic about the plan.

The veteran teachers realized that they had the opportunity to retake their college entrance exams and possibly receive higher scores. However, they were not relishing this opportunity.

African American and Hispanic American teachers examined the teacher scholarship plan. They historically had received lower college entrance exam scores than their nonminority peers. They anticipated that they would have difficulty qualifying for scholarships. They objected to the plan.

Veteran teachers, African American teachers, and Hispanic American teachers predicted that they would not qualify for scholarships. They were disgruntled. They went to the leaders of their professional union—the Florida Education Association (FEA). They asked them to investigate the characteristics of the scholarship recipients. They directed them to look for evidence of discrimination.

The FEA leaders went to the legislators. They demanded information about the scholarship recipients. They wanted to know about their ages, races, and ethnicities.

The legislators responded tersely. They explained that they had designed the scholarship program to focus on academic achievement. They did not wish to shift the focus to age, race, and ethnicity. They believed that this shift would undermine the entire program. They would not provide the data that the union wanted.

The FEA leaders represented more than one-hundred and fifty thousand members. They believed that these members were being harmed by a discriminatory program. They went to court to challenge it.

The FEA leaders also reached out to journalists for help. They told them that teachers were being denied scholarships because of flawed exams. They asked them to stir up public opposition to the scholarships.

The FEA leaders were excited when many journalists took their side in the disagreement. They were even more excited when they were joined by legions of parents.

The legislators became disconcerted by the growing opposition to their scholarship program. They consulted with the governor. They together decided to set a new course for the scholarship program.

The legislators and governor announced that they would terminate the controversial bonus program and substitute a new one. They explained that the new program would deliver a bonus to every teacher and educational administrator in Florida. They anticipated that the new program would have union support.

The FEA leaders examined the replacement program. They surprised everyone with their response to it.

The FEA leaders were pleased that the new program would reward all teachers and administrators. However, they were displeased with it for failing to reward counselors, school psychologists, applied behavior analysts, speech-language pathologists, nurses, and other professionals who worked in the schools. They stated that they were not satisfied.

GUN-CARRYING TEACHERS

Floridians were alarmed by the violence at their children's schools. They believed that it was becoming more common and more dangerous.

Floridians reached out to the groups that had pledged to reduce school violence. They contacted teachers, local school administrators, police officers, and local politicians. They had initially been optimistic that they would find a solution to the problem. However, they eventually became disappointed with them because of their scant progress.

Floridians documented the increasing violence at school. They also documented the futile efforts of educators, police officers, and local elected officials. They asked their state legislators if they could devise a solution.

The legislators assured their constituents that they would work on a solution. They reminded them that they had already taken steps to deal with dangerous assailants. They had provided the schools with funding to hire armed police officers and armed resource officers. However, they realized that these steps had been insufficient.

The legislators were not sure about the next steps that they should take. They went to school psychologists, school counselors, and school social workers. They asked for their advice.

These groups were ready to help. The psychologists explained that they could help by identifying students who were potentially dangerous. The counselors insisted that they could help by teaching potentially dangerous students to control their emotions. The social workers wanted to help by investigating whether potentially dangerous students had home lives that were contributing to dysfunctional behavior.

The legislators appreciated the advice from the educational groups. However, they were not finished gathering advice. They also met with security experts. They asked them how to improve school surveillance.

The security experts worked at commercial firms. They stated that their firms could provide devices for detecting dangerous students. They added that their firms also could provide training on how to stop dangerous students after they were detected.

The Florida legislators had listened to the advice of multiple groups. They had assured them that they valued their recommendations. However, they told them that they still needed to consult one more group—the National Rifle Association (NRA).

The Florida legislators realized that they had millions of gun-carrying constituents in their state. They knew that many of them were NRA members. They therefore asked the leaders of this organization to present their organization's views on school safety.

The NRA leaders had members who were educators. They noted that they owned guns, had concealed-carry permits, and had completed gun-safety training courses. They stated that these educators wanted to bring their guns with them to school. They were sure that they would deter armed assailants by this simple act.

The NRA leaders believed that the presence of armed educators would deter potential shooters. They explained that these educators could be trained to intervene should shooters decide to assault students, faculty, and staff.

The legislators were impressed by the NRA plan. They judged that it would be easy to implement, extremely affordable, and highly effective.

The legislators drafted a bill that authorized teachers to carry guns. They were delighted when both houses passed it and the governor signed it. They directed school districts to implement the law during the 2019–2020 academic year.

Enthusiasts

The legislators knew that their new law was controversial. They therefore let each school district decide whether to implement it. They were eager to see the response.

The legislators kept watch on the school districts at the start of the next academic year. They were pleased when eleven of the state's sixty-seven school districts announced that they were implementing the gun-carrying teacher law. They hoped that more districts would follow them.

The leaders of some school districts had been using armed teachers even before the new law went into effect. They explained that they already had the authority to hire armed guardians. They had been able to station gun-carrying teachers by appointing them as guardians.

The school leaders who had stationed gun-carrying teachers as guardians were enthusiastic about the new law. They now could station armed teachers without appointing them as guardians.

The school leaders noted that many parents in their community had been supportive of the teachers who had been serving as armed guardians. They predicted that they would be just as supportive of the new law. They were correct.

Skeptics

Florida's state legislators passed their new law in the Spring of 2019. They had been eager to see how educators would react to it.

The legislators had predicted that some educators would resist the new law. They knew that the leaders of the state's largest teacher organization, the FEA, had argued against the law while it was being debated. They expected them to remain opponents after it was enacted. They were correct.

The leaders of the FEA stated that they opposed any increase in the number of guns in schools. For this reason, they opposed arming teachers, arming school police officers, or arming school resource officers. They wanted to eliminate all armed personnel and hire more counselors, psychologists, and social workers.

The FEA leaders doubted that many teachers would be willing to carry guns after the new law was enacted. They demanded that the legislators publish the precise number of gun-carrying teachers.

The legislators refused to publish the data that the FEA had requested. They explained that these data could get into the wrong hands and then embolden assailants.

The FEA leaders were furious with the legislators. They noted that many parents believed that gun-carrying teachers would accidentally harm the children they were intending to protect. They predicted that these parents, who had sided with them before the new law was enacted, would continue to side with them.

RESPONDING TO QUESTIONS ABOUT LIMITED-DATA PROGRAMS

Legislators in Florida were distressed when extremely bright teachers turned down jobs in their state and took better-paying ones in other states. They devised a plan to keep them in Florida.

The legislators assumed that the teachers with high college entrance exam scores were the brightest. They authorized bonuses for them.

The legislators were asked to reveal the number of bonus recipients who represented minority groups. However, they refused. They contended that the data should be off limits because publicizing them would reduce the effectiveness of the teacher-bonus program.

The legislators were distressed about teachers for another reason. They worried that they were unable to protect students from armed assailants. They devised a plan to make them more formidable.

The legislators authorized teachers to carry guns at school. When they were asked to reveal the number of teachers who were carrying them, they refused. They contended that the data should be off limits because publicizing them would reduce the effectiveness of their school-safety program.

The efforts of legislators to keep teachers in Florida and to make them more formidable were unrelated. Nonetheless, they had some similarities. After you answer the following questions, see if you discern those similarities.

Question 1: Why Did Florida Legislators Award Test-Based Bonuses to Teachers?

Florida's legislators offered bonuses to teachers with high scores on college entrance exams. They assumed that they then would decline higher-salaried job offers from other states.

How did different groups respond to the legislators? Focus on two groups: teachers and parents.

Did the teachers have low confidence, moderate confidence, or high confidence in the way that the legislators were behaving? How did the parents feel? Explain the bases for your answers.

When answering these questions, as well as those that follow, you can rely on the information in this chapter. You also might rely on some of the sources that are identified in the references at the rear of the book. If you are reading this chapter with colleagues, you are encouraged to converse with them about the best way to answer the questions.

Question 2: Why Did Florida Legislators Withhold Information about Bonus Recipients?

Florida legislators were criticized because minority-group teachers historically had lower scores on college entrance exams. When they were challenged to reveal the number of minority-group participants in the teacher-bonus program, they refused. They contended that publicizing that number would divert attention to nonessential aspects of the program and reduce its effectiveness.

How did different groups respond to the legislators? Focus on two groups: teachers and parents.

Did the teachers have low confidence, moderate confidence, or high confidence in the way that the legislators were behaving? How did the parents feel? Explain the bases for your answers.

Question 3: Why Did Florida Legislators Authorize Teachers to Carry Guns?

Florida's legislators authorized teachers to carry guns at school. They believed that they then would be able to prevent weapon-carrying assailants from harming students.

How did different groups respond to the legislators? Focus on two groups: teachers and parents.

Did the teachers have low confidence, moderate confidence, or high confidence in the way that the legislators were behaving? How did the parents feel? Explain the bases for your answers.

Question 4: Why Did Florida Legislators Withhold Information about Gun-Carrying Teachers?

Florida legislators were criticized because teachers historically had shown little enthusiasm for carrying guns. When they were challenged to reveal the number of participants in the teacher-arming program, they refused. They contended that publicizing that number would embolden assailants and reduce the effectiveness of the program.

How did different groups respond to the legislators? Focus on two groups: teachers and parents.

Did the teachers have low confidence, moderate confidence, or high confidence in the way that the legislators were behaving? How did the parents feel? Explain the bases for your answers.

SUMMARY

Florida's legislators wished to retain bright teachers. They authorized bonuses for those with high test scores. They then were challenged to reveal the number of bonus recipients who represented minority groups.

Florida's legislators wished to make teachers more formidable against assailants. They authorized them to carry guns at school. They then were challenged to reveal the number of teachers who were carrying guns.

Chapter 12

How Effective Are Rap Music Bans?

[A] criticism of rap music . . . is that it can incite imminent lawless action.

—Law Professor David Hudson, 2020

[Rap music heralds] violence, drugs, guns, killing, ignorance, misogyny, and everything base.

—Parent Denise Williams, 2019

[We have banned rap music on school buses] to limit student exposure to . . . profanity and violent lyrics.

—Portland Public Schools Spokeswoman Courtney Westling, 2016

[Portland's anti-rap-music] policy is overtly racist.

—Parent Colleen Ryan-Onken, 2016

Executives at Patagonia railed against environmental exploitation. They banned sales of corporate sportswear to firms that were culpable. They wondered how customers would respond.

Portland's educational administrators railed against music that extolled violence. Convinced that rap music was culpable, they banned it from their schools' buildings, grounds, and busses. They wondered how parents would respond.

RESTRICTING CORPORATE CLOTHING SALES

Yvon Chouinard was a mid-twentieth-century sports enthusiast. He especially loved rock climbing.

Although Chouinard loved his sport, he did not love the rock climbing sportswear for which he had to settle. He criticized it as uncomfortable, non-durable, and unstylish. He added that it had been produced with techniques that demonstrated little respect for the environment.

Chouinard established his own sportswear firm—Patagonia. He promised that he would use environmentally friendly techniques to create high-quality apparel. He hired a cadre of executives who shared his philosophy.

The executives at Patagonia were convinced that their founder's philosophy was good for the environment. They believed that it also was good for sales. They beamed as it helped their firm grow into a billion-dollar enterprise.

The executives wished to share the Patagonia philosophy with a wider audience. They experimented with several promotional strategies.

The executives imposed a one percent surcharge on their products. They then donated that revenue to organizations that opposed environmental exploitation. They featured these organizations in a special section on their corporate website.

The executives devised another attention-grabbing promotional strategy. They allowed customers to return old Patagonia items and get credit that they could use to secure the latest items. They then refurbished the returned items and resold them as vintage sports garments.

The executives devised still another ingenious promotional strategy. They had been producing customized vests that were embellished with the logos of Wall Street finance firms. They announced that they would ban sales of these garments to firms that had violated Patagonia's philosophy.

Enthusiasts

The Patagonia executives waited to see how their customers were responding to their promotional strategies. They were particularly keen to see their reaction to the restrictions on sales of corporate sportswear. They were gratified when their customers signaled approval.

The executives wondered if the leaders of other sportswear corporations would copy their strong pro-environmental stance. They were excited when they did. They assumed that they were validating the Patagonia philosophy.

The executives had the support of customers and fellow corporate leaders. They smiled as this support grew. They beamed as sales also grew.

Skeptics

The executives were pleased with Patagonia's philosophy. They credited it with protecting the environment and attracting new customers. Nonetheless, they acknowledged that it had disappointed some customers.

The disappointed customers contended that the Patagonia executives had complex motives. They conceded that they were taking steps to increase environmentalism. However, they pointed out that they also were taking steps to increase profits.

The skeptical consumers looked for an instance in which the executives had to choose between increasing environmentalism and increasing profits. They quickly found a case.

The executives had been marketing garments made from sheared wool. However, they had to deal with environmental activists, who highlighted the pain that shearing caused to the sheep.

The executives had chosen to stick with sheared wool garments and ignore the pain from shearing. Although they later reversed their decision, they did so only after whistleblowers had created harmful publicity.

RESTRICTING RAP MUSIC

Many black youths had faced daunting challenges during the 1970s. Those who resided in inner-city neighborhoods had to deal with practical and psychological problems. They had to deal with the practical problems associated with staying safe. They had to deal with the psychological problems associated with discrimination.

The disenfranchised black youths had feelings of dejection, resentment, and anger. They looked for a way to vent those feelings. Some of them turned to music.

This was not the first era in which African Americans had expressed their feelings through music. They historically had relied on folk music, jazz, gospel, and the blues. During the 1970s, they were searching for a new musical outlet. They began to rap.

The early rappers created lyrics about crime, drugs, poverty, police, jail, sex, exploitation, alcohol, and violence. They paired them with stark and haunting rhythms.

The rappers immediately found passionate followers in New York City. They attracted them in other cities as well. They soon had legions of national and international admirers.

Some fans referred to the new musicians as hip-hop artists. Others simply labeled them rappers.

School administrators were aware of rap music. They had heard students playing it on loud portable devices that they carried through school buildings, on schoolgrounds, and in school buses.

The administrators had to decide how to handle rap music. Some of them were nonchalant about it. They told students that they could listen to it if they did not disrupt classes.

Some administrators were enthusiastic about rap music. They incorporated it into their curricula. They directed their teachers to make it the pretext for heady musical discussions and profound social dialogues.

The administrators in the Portland Public School District had a different reaction to rap music. They certainly did not wish to embrace it. In fact, they did not even wish to signal tacit approval. They believed that it had too many problems.

The administrators disapproved of rap music when it was played on equipment that had loud and reverberating speakers. They objected to it because it disrupted school functions. However, they objected to it even when it was played quietly. They contended that it had lyrics that could incite students to violence.

The Portland administrators had clear safety policies. They made them the basis for their decision to ban rap music within school buildings and on schoolgrounds.

The administrators had taken care of rap music in their buildings and on their grounds. However, they later realized that they had not addressed it on school buses.

The administrators reviewed their current school transportation policies. They noted that they did not forbid students from playing music on school buses. They resolved to modify those policies.

The administrators amended their school bus policies in 2016. They explained the new policies still permitted students to play music on the buses. However, they forbade them from playing rap music on them.

Enthusiasts

The administrators knew that students had been playing rap music on buses. They were able to anticipate how they would react to the new school bus policy. They were sure that they would be miffed.

The administrators were interested in how riders who did not play rap music would react to the new policy. They assumed that some of them found rap disconcerting. They hoped that they would be supportive of the ban. However, they were wrong.

Students resented the new policy. They did not want school administrators choosing their music. They preferred to choose it on their own.

The administrators were extremely interested in how parents would react to their ban on rap music. They were gratified when some of them expressed support.

The supportive parents identified court cases in which prosecutors had attempted to incriminate suspects based on the music to which they listened. They noted that these prosecutors, who had focused on rap music with violent lyrics, discerned a link between that music and acts of violence. They concluded that music of this sort had no place in Portland schools.

Skeptics

Some parents supported Portland's ban on rap music. However, they were outnumbered by the parents who opposed it.

The skeptical parents asked the administrators why they had focused so intently on rap music. They noted that other musical genres had violent lyrics. They gave examples from country, Latino, and rock music.

The administrators insisted that they had not exclusively banned rap music. They explained that they also had banned political radio programs and Christian radio programs. They hoped that this information would appease the parents.

The parents were not appeased. They conceded that some of the bus drivers might be listening to political talk shows or Christian radio stations. However, they doubted that any of the students were listening to them. They concluded that the students were being affected exclusively by the rap music ban.

The angry parents believed that the administrators had designed their bus policy poorly. They suggested that they replace it with a policy like that which some schools had adopted for violent video games. These schools had not banned violent games. They instead had encouraged parents to discuss these games with their children.

The angry parents believed that Portland's rap-music policy was racist. They also believed that it was ineffective. They contacted journalists and asked them to publicize their discontent. They were excited when the journalists responded with passion.

The administrators had kept a watch on parents. They were disheartened by those who opposed their rap music policy. However, they had two more groups that they were watching—elected officials and the leaders in other school districts. They hoped that these groups would give them the support that they needed to keep their ban in place. They became truly disheartened when both groups expressed skepticism.

RESPONDING TO QUESTIONS ABOUT CONTROVERSIAL RESTRICTIONS

Executives at Patagonia wished to publicize their opposition to environmental exploitation. They donated one percent of their profits to anti-exploitation organizations. They later amplified their campaign: they refused to sell customized corporate sportswear to firms that were exploitative.

School administrators in Portland wished to publicize their opposition to music that extolled violence. Convinced that rap music was culpable, they banned it from school buildings and grounds. They later amplified their campaign: they banned it from school buses.

The attempts to publicly denounce environmental exploitation and violent music were unrelated. Nonetheless, they had some similarities. As you answer the following questions, see if you discern those similarities.

Question 1: How Did Patagonia Executives Publicize their Opposition to Environmental Exploitation?

Patagonia executives wished to publicize their opposition to environmental exploitation. They donated one percent of their profits to anti-exploitation organizations.

How did different groups respond to the Patagonia executives? Focus on two groups: the leaders at other sportswear firms and consumers.

Did the leaders at other sportswear firms have low confidence, moderate confidence, or high confidence in the way that the Patagonia executives were behaving? How did consumers feel? Explain the bases for your answers.

When answering these questions, you can rely on the information in this chapter. You also might rely on some of the sources that are identified in the references at the rear of the book. If you are reading this chapter with colleagues, you are encouraged to converse with them about the best way to answer the questions.

Question 2: How Did Patagonia Executives Intensify their Opposition to Environmental Exploitation?

Patagonia executives concluded that their one percent tax had only a limited impact. They went a step further: they banned sales of customized corporate sportswear to firms that exploited the environment.

How did different groups respond to the Patagonia executives? Focus on two groups: the leaders at other sportswear firms and consumers.

Did the leaders at other sportswear firms have low confidence, moderate confidence, or high confidence in the way that the Patagonia executives were behaving? How did consumers feel? Explain the bases for your answers.

Question 3: How Did Portland Educational Administrators Publicize their Opposition to Rap Music?

Educational administrators in Portland wished to publicize their opposition to music that extolled violence. Convinced that rap music was culpable, they banned it from their school buildings and grounds.

How did diverse groups respond to these educational administrators? Focus on two groups: parents and students.

Did the parents have low confidence, moderate confidence, or high confidence in the way that Portland's educational administrators were behaving? How did the students feel? Explain the bases for your answers.

Question 4: How Did Portland Educational Administrators Intensify their Opposition to Rap Music?

Portland's educational administrators concluded that banning rap music from school buildings and school grounds had only a limited impact. They went a step further: they banned it from school buses.

How did diverse groups respond to these educational administrators? Focus on two groups: parents and students.

Did the parents have low confidence, moderate confidence, or high confidence in the way that Portland's educational administrators were behaving? How did the students feel? Explain the bases for your answers.

SUMMARY

Executives at Patagonia denounced environmental exploitation. They refused to sell their customized corporate sportswear to firms that were culpable. They were eager to see the impact of their ban.

Educational administrators in Portland denounced music that extolled violence. Convinced that rap music was culpable, they banned it from school buildings, grounds, and buses. They were eager to see the impact of their ban.

Bibliography

PREFACE

References for Preface Epigraphs

Florida Grand Jury.—*quoted by* Ceballos, A. (2020, January 11). Florida grapples with school safety. *Florida Times-Union.* Retrieved from: http://digital.olivesoftware.com/Olive/ODN/FloridaTimesUnion/shared/ShowArticle.aspx?doc=TFTU%2F2020%2F01%2F11&entity=Ar00109&sk=E59450BB&mode=text.

Jones, B.—*quoted by* De Leon, J. (2019, February 7). Palmetto principal has a warning for school shooters: "We are going to put them down." *Bradenton Herald.* Retrieved from: https://www.bradenton.com/news/local/article225203920.html.

Jones, W.—*quoted by* Bloch, E. (2020, March 17). Tax vote may be stalled by virus. *Florida Times-Union.* Retrieved from: http://digital.olivesoftware.com/Olive/ODN/FloridaTimesUnion/shared/ShowArticle.aspx?doc=TFTU%2F2020%2F03%2F17&entity=Ar00901&sk=5D17806F&mode=text.

Rowan, J. (2020, March 15). Put Jacksonville back on track, recall Curry. *Florida Times-Union.* Retrieved from: http://digital.olivesoftware.com/Olive/ODN/FloridaTimesUnion/shared/ShowArticle.aspx?doc=TFTU%2F2020%2F03%2F15&entity=Ar03900&sk=1B7D20F8&mode=text.

Schamis, I. (2020, February 16). It's not enough to remember Parkland shooting. *Florida Times-Union.* Retrieved from: http://digital.olivesoftware.com/Olive/ODN/FloridaTimesUnion/shared/ShowArticle.aspx?doc=TFTU%2F2020%2F02%2F16&entity=Ar03601&sk=7F8C1AA1&mode=text.

Whitcher, C. (2019, November 16). Pediatrician's anti-gun views don't offer practical solutions. *Florida Times-Union.* Retrieved from: http://digital.olivesoftware.com/Olive/ODN/FloridaTimesUnion/shared/ShowArticle.aspx?doc=TFTU%2F2019%2F11%2F16&entity=Ar01302&sk=2D0E9364&mode=text.

CHAPTER 1

References for Chapter 1 Epigraphs

Florida Times-Union Editorial Board. (2020, February 14). Leading on smart justice. *Florida Times-Union*. Retrieved from: http://digital.olivesoftware.com/Olive/ODN/FloridaTimesUnion/shared/ShowArticle.aspx?doc=TFTU%2F2020%2F02%2F14&entity=Ar00601&sk=0BAFDE42&mode=text.

Gottfredson, D.—*quoted by* Eckholm, E (2013, April 12). With police in schools, more children in court. *New York Times*. Retrieved from: https://www.nytimes.com/2013/04/12/education/with-police-in-schools-more-children-in-court.html.

Fox, J. A., & Rich-Shea, A. M. (2020, June 12). Don't defund all police, but keep police out of schools. *USA TODAY*. Retrieved from: https://www.usatoday.com/story/opinion/2020/06/12/defund-school-police-obstacles-to-student-success-column/5336791002.

New York Times Editorial Board. (2013, April 18). Criminalizing children at school. *New York Times*. Retrieved from: https://www.nytimes.com/2013/04/19/opinion/criminalizing-children-at-school.html.

Rolle, K.—*quoted by* Zaveri, M. (2020, February 27). Body camera footage shows arrest by Orlando police of 6-year-old at school. *New York Times*. Retrieved from: https://www.nytimes.com/2020/02/27/us/orlando-6-year-old-arrested.html.

References for Expelling Professors—Introduction

Furfaro, H. (2019, December 26). In hopes of ending enrollment woes, the Evergreen State College is overhauling its academic programs. *Seattle Times*. Retrieved from: https://www.seattletimes.com/education-lab/in-hopes-of-ending-enrollment-woes-evergreen-state-college-is-overhauling-its-academic-programs.

Wall Street Journal Editorial Board. (2019, September 30). A Judicial Primer on Bias Response. *Wall Street Journal*. Retrieved from: https://www.wsj.com/articles/a-judicial-primer-on-bias-response-11569786160.

References for Expelling Professors—Enthusiasts

Fischel, A., Grossman, Z., &, Nelson, L. (2017, August 11). Another side of the Evergreen State College story. *Huffington Post*. Retrieved from: https://www.huffpost.com/entry/evergreen-state-college-another-side_b_598cd293e4b090964295e8fc.

Hartocollis, A. (2017, June 16). A campus argument goes viral: Now the college is under siege. *New York Times*. Retrieved from: https://www.nytimes.com/2017/06/16/us/evergreen-state-protests.html.

Signer, M. (2020, March 13). How free speech dogma failed us in Charlottesville. *Wall Street Journal*. Retrieved from: https://www.wsj.com/articles/how-free-speech-dogma-failed-us-in-charlottesville-11584108766.

Weinstein, B. (2017, May 30). The campus mob came for me—and you, professor, could be next. *Wall Street Journal*. Retrieved from: https://www.wsj.com/articles/the-campus-mob-came-for-meand-you-professor-could-be-next-1496187482.

References for Expelling Professors—Skeptics

Parke, C. (2018, September 12). Evergreen State sees "catastrophic" drop in enrollment after social justice meltdown. Foxnews.com. Retrieved from: https://www.foxnews.com/us/evergreen-state-sees-catastrophic-drop-in-enrollment-after-social-justice-meltdown.

Richardson, B. (2017, May 27). College professor Bret Weinstein holds class off campus, citing students threatening violence. *Washington Times*. Retrieved from: https://www.washingtontimes.com/news/2017/may/27/bret-weinstein-evergreen-state-professor-holds-cla.

References for Expelling Students—Introduction

Bagley, N. (2019, July 31). Crime, violence, discipline, and safety in U.S. public schools. National Center for Education Statistics. Retrieved from: https://youthtoday.org/2019/07/crime-violence-discipline-and-safety-in-u-s-public-schoolss.

Duxbury, L., & Bennell, C. (2020). *Police in schools: An evidence-based look at the use of school resource officers*. New York: Routledge.

Nolan, K., & Willis, P. (2011). *Police in the hallways: Discipline in an urban high school*. Minneapolis: University of Minnesota Press.

Rhee, N. (2019, November 11). For Chicago kids shaken by gun violence, a shortage of trauma support compounds the harm. Thetrace.org. Retrieved from: https://www.thetrace.org/2019/11/for-chicago-kids-shaken-by-gun-violence-a-shortage-of-trauma-support-compounds-the-harm.

References for Expelling Students—Enthusiasts

American Civil Liberties Union. (2020). Smart justice. Aclu.org. Retrieved from https://www.aclu.org/issues/smart-justice.

Chen, G. (2019, September 30). Cops and children: Why police officers are stationed at elementary schools. Publicschoolreview.com. Retrieved from: https://www.publicschoolreview.com/blog/cops-and-children-why-police-officers-are-stationed-at-elementary-schools.

Coble, C. (2019, September 25). Can you get arrested in elementary school? Findlaw.com. Retrieved from: https://blogs.findlaw.com/blotter/2019/09/can-you-get-arrested-in-elementary-school.html.

Deakin, J., Taylor, E., & Kupchik, A. (Eds.). (2018). *The Palgrave international handbook of school discipline, surveillance, and social control*. New York: Palgrave Macmillan.

Eckholm, E. (2013, April 12). With police in schools, more children in court. *New York Times*. Retrieved from: https://www.nytimes.com/2013/04/12/education/with-police-in-schools-more-children-in-court.html.

Fox, J. A., & Rich-Shea, A. M. (2020, June 12). Don't defund all police, but keep police out of schools. *USA TODAY*. Retrieved from: https://www.usatoday.com/story/opinion/2020/06/12/defund-school-police-obstacles-to-student-success-column/5336791002.

Hollow, M. C. (2020, February 27). When the police stop a teenager with special needs. *New York Times*. Retrieved from: https://www.nytimes.com/2020/02/27/well/family/autism-special-needs-police.html.

New York State School Boards Association. (2019, December 3). Armed security in schools: What the research says. Nyssba.org. Retrieved from: https://www.nyssba.org/clientuploads/nyssba_pdf/Reports/armed-security-report-12032019.pdf.

References for Expelling Students—Skeptics

Ohm, R. (2020, March 5). Pros and cons of school policing are debated at Portland forum. *Portland Press Herald*. Retrieved from: https://www.pressherald.com/2020/03/05/pros-and-cons-of-school-policing-debated-at-portland-forum.

Policing America's schools. (2017). Which students are arrested the most? *Education Week*. Retrieved from: https://www.edweek.org/ew/projects/2017/policing-americas-schools/student-arrests.html#/overview.

Raghavendran, B. (2017, May 24). Police in schools: Minneapolis school board weighs pros and cons. *Star Tribune*. Retrieved from: https://www.startribune.com/cops-in-schools-minneapolis-school-board-weighs-pros-and-cons/424071693/.

Superville, D. R. (2019, December 11). Most principals have no say in choosing police for their schools. *Education Week*. Retrieved from: https://www.edweek.org/ew/articles/2019/12/11/most-principals-have-no-say-in-choosing.html.

Whirty, R. (2019, June 3). Lack of resources plays role in funneling students with disabilities through school-to-prison pipeline. *Louisiana Weekly*. Retrieved from: http://www.louisianaweekly.com/lack-of-resources-plays-role-in-funneling-students-with-disabilities-through-school-to-prison-pipeline.

Whitaker, A., Torres-Guillén, S., Morton, M., Jordan, H., Coyle, S., Mann, A., & Sun, W. L. (2019). *Cops and no counselors: How the lack of school mental health staff is harming students*. New York: American Civil Liberties Union.

Zaveri, M. (2020, February 27). Body camera footage shows arrest by Orlando police of 6-year-old at school. *New York Times*. Retrieved from: https://www.nytimes.com/2020/02/27/us/orlando-6-year-old-arrested.html.

CHAPTER 2

References for Chapter 2 Epigraphs

Bethel School District. (2016). School safety. Author. Retrieved from: http://www.bethel.k12.or.us/district/school-safety.

Canan, P.—*quoted by* Kelley, C. (2019, October 24). Fewer active shooter drills proposed. *Florida Times-Union*. Retrieved from: http://digital.olivesoftware.com/Olive/ODN/FloridaTimesUnion/shared/ShowArticle.aspx?doc=TFTU%2F2019%2F10%2F24&entity=Ar01319&sk=51F1D3B1&mode=text.

Littleton Public Schools. (2020). School safety protocols. Author. Retrieved from: https://littletonpublicschools.net/school-safety-protocols.

Perry, B.—quoted by Williamson, E. (2019, September 4). When active-shooter drills scare the children they hope to protect. *New York Times*. Retrieved from: https://www.nytimes.com/2019/09/04/us/politics/active-shooter-drills-schools.html.

References for Shocking Political Videos—Introduction

Morris, B. (2020, January 7). Facebook bans deep fakes but permits some altered content. *Wall Street Journal*. Retrieved from: https://www.wsj.com/articles/facebooks-deepfake-video-ban-permits-some-altered-content-11578384519.

Roose, K. (2018, March 4). Here come the fake videos, too. *New York Times*. Retrieved from: https://www.nytimes.com/2018/03/04/technology/fake-videos-deepfakes.html.

Watercutter. A. (2019, December 5). The Irishman gets de-aging right—No tracking dots necessary. *Wired*. Retrieved from: https://www.wired.com/story/the-irishman-netflix-ilm-de-aging.

References for Shocking Political Videos—Enthusiasts

Ember, S. (2019, April 4). Trump tweets doctored video mocking Joe Biden. *New York Times*. Retrieved from: https://www.nytimes.com/2019/04/04/us/politics/trump-biden-tweet-meme.html.

Grynbaum, M. M., & Williamson, E. (2018, November 8). Trump Administration uses misleading video to justify barring of CNN's Jim Acosta. *New York Times*. Retrieved from: https://www.nytimes.com/2018/11/08/business/media/infowars-white-house-jim-acosta-cnn.html.

Mervosh, S. (2019, May 24). Distorted videos of Nancy Pelosi spread on Facebook and Twitter, helped by Trump. *New York Times*. Retrieved from: https://www.nytimes.com/2019/05/24/us/politics/pelosi-doctored-video.html.

Shane, S., & Blinder, A. (2018, December 19). Secret experiment in Alabama senate race imitated Russian tactics. *New York Times*. Retrieved from: https://www.nytimes.com/2018/12/19/us/alabama-senate-roy-jones-russia.html.

References for Shocking Political Videos—Skeptics

Grynbaum, M. M. (2017, July 2). Trump tweets a video of him wrestling "CNN" to the ground. *New York Times*. Retrieved from: https://www.nytimes.com/2017/07/02/business/media/trump-wrestling-video-cnn-twitter.html.

Tyler, A. (2019, December 5). The Irishman shows the limits of CGI deaging [*sic*]. Screenrant.com. Retrieved from: https://screenrant.com/irishman-movie-netflix-cgi-deaging-actors-limits-bad.

References for Shocking School Videos—Introduction

Means, S. P. (2019, August 30). Utah launches firearms safety video for schools, confronting "the reality that guns are part of our society." *Salt Lake City Tribune*. Retrieved from: https://www.sltrib.com/news/education/2019/08/29/utah-launches-firearms.

Safer schools for our kids. (2108). Secondary safety video: What to do in the case of a school shooter (video). Saferschoolsforourkids.org. Retrieved from: https://www.saferschoolsforourkids.org/videos.

School safety videos. (2020). safetyvideos.com. Retrieved from: https://www.safetyvideos.com/Safety_Training_Videos_For_Schools_s/44.htm.

Williamson, E. (2019, September 4). When active-shooter drills scare the children they hope to protect. *New York Times*. Retrieved from: https://www.nytimes.com/2019/09/04/us/politics/active-shooter-drills-schools.html.

References for Shocking School Videos—Enthusiasts

Gajanan, M. (2019, September 18). Gun violence prevention group releases "Back to School": PSA video showing the reality of school shootings from students' perspectives. *Time*. Retrieved from: https://time.com/5680120/sandy-hook-promise-school-shooting-psa/.

National School Safety and Security Services. (2020). School threat assessment training: Assessing and managing school threats. Author. Retrieved from: https://www.schoolsecurity.org/school-safety-and-communications-services/school-threat-assessment-training-assessing-managing-school-threats.

References for Shocking School Videos—Skeptics

Blad, E. (2017, September 19). Do schools' "active-shooter" drills prepare or frighten? *Education Week*. Retrieved from: https://www.edweek.org/ew/articles/2017/09/20/do-schools-active-shooter-drills-prepare-or-frighten.html.

O'Regan, S. V. (2019, December 13). The company behind America's scariest school shooter drills. Thetrace.org. Retrieved from: https://www.thetrace.org/2019/12/alice-active-shooter-training-school-safety/.

School shootings: Sandy Hook parents' haunting video warning. (2019, September 19). Bbc.com. Retrieved from: https://www.bbc.com/news/newsbeat-49751150.

Tavel, J. (2018, August 20). After parents object, Pinellas halts active shooter training videos for younger kids. *Tampa Bay Times*. Retrieved from: https://www.tampabay.com/news/education/k12/After-parents-object-Pinellas-halts-active-shooter-training-videos-for-younger-kids_171061626.

CHAPTER 3

References for Chapter 3 Epigraphs

ArmorMe. (2018). Tested by security experts. Author. Retrieved from: https://www.armorme.com.

Drury, J.—*quoted by* Reagan, C. (2019, August 6). Bulletproof backpacks have become another back-to-school staple. Cnbc.com. Retrieved from: https://www.cnbc.com/2019/08/06/bullet-resistant-backpacks-have-become-another-back-to-school-staple.html.

Guard Dog Security. (2020). Practical bulletproof backpacks. Guarddog-security.com. Retrieved from: https://guarddog-security.com/practical-bulletproof-backpacks.

Meredith, K. (2019. September 6). As kids go back to school, 47% of parents show interest in bulletproof backpacks. Morningconsult.com. Retrieved from: https://morningconsult.com/2019/09/06/as-kids-go-back-to-school-47-of-parents-show-interest-in-bulletproof-backpacks.

Unidentified North Carolina Parent.—*quoted by* Yaffe-Bellany, D. (2019, August 6). Bulletproof backpacks in demand for back-to-school shopping. *New York Times*. Retrieved from: https://www.nytimes.com/2019/08/06/business/bulletproof-backpack.html.

References for No-Cost Marketing—Introduction

Nike's advertising and promotion costs from 2014 to 2019. (2020). Statista.com. Retrieved from: https://www.statista.com/statistics/685734/nike-ad-spend.

Nyitray, B. (2020, January 27). Are Nike's Vaporfly running shoes "too good?" Fool.com. Retrieved from: https://www.fool.com/investing/2020/01/27/are-nike-vaporfly-running-shoes-too-good.aspx.

Quealy, K., & Katz, J. (2018, July 18). Nike says its $250 running shoes will make you run much faster: What if that's actually true? *New York Times*. Retrieved from: https://www.nytimes.com/interactive/2018/07/18/upshot/nike-vaporfly-shoe-strava.html.

Roe, D. (2020, February 6). Every reason to hate on the Nike Alphafly, ranked. *Runners World*. Retrieved from: https://www.runnersworld.com/gear/a30796818/nike-alphafly-debate.

Safdar, K., & Bachman, R. (2020, February 5). Nike Alphafly sneakers will also avoid Olympic ban. *Wall Street Journal*. Retrieved from: https://www.wsj.com/articles/nike-alphafly-sneakers-will-also-avoid-olympic-ban-11580929200.

References for No-Cost Marketing—Enthusiasts

Safdar, K., & Bachman, R. (2020, February 28). Nike's offer to U.S. Olympic marathon trials runners: Free shoes. *Wall Street Journal*. Retrieved from: https://www.wsj.com/articles/nikes-offer-to-u-s-olympic-marathon-trials-runners-free-shoes-11582894728.

Stewart, J. (2020, January 30). Is the highly engineered Nike Vaporfly just a shoe? Marketplace.org. Retrieved from: https://www.marketplace.org/shows/marketplace-tech/is-the-highly-engineered-nike-vaporfly-just-a-shoe.

References for No-Cost Marketing—Skeptics

Balu, N., Venugopal, A., Sridhar, S., Fares, M., & Wallis, D. (2020, January 17). Why a ban on Vaporfly shoe could boost Nike's bottom line. Businessoffashion.com. Retrieved from: https://www.businessoffashion.com/articles/news-analysis/why-a-ban-on-vaporfly-shoe-could-boost-nikes-bottom-line.

La Monica, P. R. (2018, September 5). Nike investors aren't happy about the Colin Kaepernick ad. Cnn.com. Retrieved from: https://money.cnn.com/2018/09/04/news/companies/nike-stock-down-colin-kaepernick/index.html.

Pasquarelli, A., & Schultz, E.J. (2018, September 7). Shoe burners flameout: Nike's Kaepernick ad led to sales uptick. Adage.com. Retrieved from: http://adage.com/article/cmo-strategy/nike-s-kaepernick-ad-led-sales-uptick/314859.

References for No-Cost School Safety—Introduction

D'Innocenzio, A. (2019, August 10). "Times have changed": Mass shootings give rise to bullet-resistant backpacks. *Florida Times-Union*. Retrieved from: http://digital.olivesoftware.com/Olive/ODN/FloridaTimesUnion/shared/ShowArticle.aspx?doc=TFTU%2F2019%2F08%2F10&entity=Ar01403&sk=FC907F64&mode=text.

Giordano, G. (2012a). *Capping costs: Putting a price tag on school reform*. Lanham, MD: Rowman & Littlefield.

Giordano, G. (2012b). *Teachers go to rehab: Historical and current advice to instructors*. Lanham, MD: Rowman & Littlefield.

Giordano, G. (2015). *Commonsense questions about school administration: The answers can provide essential steps to improvement*. Lanham, MD: Rowman & Littlefield.

Giordano, G. (2020). *Parents and school tech: Answers reveal essential steps to improvement*. Lanham, MD: Rowman & Littlefield.

Strauss, V. (2019, August 2). "This is our sad reality": Bulletproof backpacks are a big back-to-school item. *Washington Post*. Retrieved from: https://www.washingtonpost.com/education/2019/08/02/this-is-our-sad-reality-bulletproof-backpacks-are-big-back-to-school-item/.

Yaffe-Bellany, D. (2019, August 6). Bulletproof backpacks in demand for back-to-school shopping. *New York Times*. Retrieved from: https://www.nytimes.com/2019/08/06/business/bulletproof-backpack.html.

References for No-Cost School Safety—Enthusiasts

Body Armor. (2020). AR500 Armor® Level III Backpack Armor 9.5" x 13." Retrieved from: https://www.ar500armor.com/ar500-armor-backpack-plate.html?gclid=EAIaIQobChMIuZLfvra66AIVjIrICh3QCwn5EAkYEyABEgIptvD_BwE.

Florida school shooting students told to wear clear backpacks. (2018, March 22). Bbc.com. Retrieved from: https://www.bbc.com/news/newsbeat-43499045.

Harrington, J. (2020, January 6). How school backpacks have changed over the last few decades. Wallst.com. Retrieved from: https://247wallst.com/special-report/2019/09/13/how-school-backbacks-have-changed-over-the-last-few-decades/2/.

Holder, S. (2019, November 6). The empty promise of the clear plastic backpack. Citylab.com. Retrieved from: https://www.citylab.com/life/2019/11/clear-plastic-backpack-bags-safety-school-shootings-security/600310.

References for No-Cost School Safety—Skeptics

Popken, B. (2019, August 21). Bulletproof backpacks wouldn't have saved anyone in recent shootings. Nbcnews.com. Retrieved from: https://www.nbcnews.com/business/consumer/bulletproof-backpacks-wouldn-t-have-saved-anyone-recent-shootings-n1042801.

Reed, S. (2018, March 22). How did transparent bags become the solution to gun violence? *Hollywood Reporter*. Retrieved from: https://www.hollywoodreporter.com/news/how-did-transparent-bags-become-solution-gun-violence-1096620.

Safe Life Defense. (2020). Backpack Armor. Retrieved from: https://safelifedefense.com/product/backpack-armor-panel/?gclid=EAIaIQobChMIuZLfvra66AIVjIrICh3QCwn5EAkYDiABEgJ_9vD_BwE.

Taylor E. (2013). *Surveillance schools: A new era in education*. Palgrave Pivot, London.

CHAPTER 4

References for Chapter 4 Epigraphs

Centegix. (2020). CrisisAlert. Author. Retrieved from: https://go.centegix.com/l/747993/2020-02-21/244fh?gclid=EAIaIQobChMI-cGmi5n15wIVA1YMCh0FcwOBEAMYASAAEgKHr_D_BwE.

Florida Senate. (2020). Florida Senate Bill 70: Alert systems in public schools. Author. Retrieved from: https://sonitrolsecurity.com/panic-button-in-your-school/https://www.flsenate.gov/Session/Bill/2020/70.

Kimberline Corporation. (2020). Why you need panic buttons in your school. Author. Retrieved from: https://sonitrolsecurity.com/panic-button-in-your-school/.

Murphy, P.—*quoted by* Moran, R. (2019, February 6). Murphy signs law for "panic alarms" to improve N.J. school safety. *Philadelphia Inquirer*. Retrieved from:

https://www.inquirer.com/news/new-jersey-alyssa-parkland-shooting-panic-alarm-schools-20190207.html.

O'Loughlin, T.—quoted by Lewis, B. (2014, July). Panic button app allows silent communication. Schoolsafetyinfo.org. Retrieved from: https://www.schoolsafetyinfo.org/stories/Success4Milford-Panic-Button.html.

Silent Beacon Company. (2021). Silent beacon personal safety device. Silentbeacon.com. Retrieved from: https://silentbeacon.com/product/personal-safety-device-store.

References for Money-Saving Meals—Introduction

Choi, C. (2019, May 17). How "lunch shaming" is facing scrutiny around the US. *Florida Times-Union*. Retrieved from: http://digital.olivesoftware.com/Olive/ODN/FloridaTimesUnion/shared/ShowArticle.aspx?doc=TFTU%2F2019%2F05%2F17&entity=Ar03402&sk=5C9E5E25&mode=text.

Food Research and Action Center. (2021). National School Lunch Program. Retrieved from: https://frac.org/wp-content/uploads/cnnslp.pdf.

United States Department of Agriculture. (2021). National School Lunch Program. Author. https://www.fns.usda.gov/nslp.

References for Money-Saving Meals—Enthusiasts

Adely, H. (2019, November 13). Schools "in a bind": Here are the decisions facing NJ schools as lunch debt becomes growing issue. Retrieved from: https://www.northjersey.com/story/news/education/2019/11/07/lunch-debt-rising-nj-creating-controversy-over-lunch-shaming/4124949002.

Long, H. (2017, May 10). School lunch shaming: Inside America's hidden debt crisis. Cnn.com. Retrieved from: https://money.cnn.com/2017/05/09/news/economy/school-lunch-shaming-debt-crisis/index.html.

Moreau, W., & Pilcher, J. (2020). The incentives behind lunch shaming. American Bar Association. Retrieved from: https://www.americanbar.org/groups/young_lawyers/publications/tyl/topics/access-to-education/incentives-behind-lunch-shaming/.

References for Money-Saving Meals—Skeptics

Quinn, M. (2019, September). Shamed in the lunch line. Governing.com. Retrieved from: https://www.governing.com/topics/education/gov-lunch-shaming.html.

Tully, T., & Schweber, N. (2019, November 7). First, the tuna fish "badge of shame." *New York Times*. Retrieved from: https://www.nytimes.com/2019/11/01/nyregion/cherry-hill-lunch-elizabeth-warren.html.

References for Money-Saving Safety Devices—Introduction

Alyssa's Law in Florida: Answers to your questions. (2021). Schoolmessenger.com. Retrieved from: https://www.schoolmessenger.com/alyssas-law-florida?gclid=CjwKCAjwjJmIBhA4EiwAQdCbxu1dCKmqdUIqxT8aPe02FIRaORdDBQozhnwRCpbj_W-EX5ze6HsMMBoChGAQAvD_BwE.

Campo-Flores, A. (2020, January 12). Florida considers panic alarms for schools to respond to shootings. *Wall Street Journal*. Retrieved from: https://www.wsj.com/articles/florida-considers-panic-alarms-for-schools-to-respond-to-shootings-11578830400.

Enseo's MadeSafe Alert System for education enhances student safety at Lovejoy Independent School District. (2018, August 20). Enseo.com. Retrieved from: https://enseo.com/press-releases/2018/08/20/enseos-madesafe-alert-system-for-education-enhances-student-safety-at-lovejoy-independent-school-district.

Florida Department of Education. (2021). Funding & allocations. Author. Retrieved from: https://www.fldoe.org/safe-schools/funding-allocations.stml.

Herold, B. (|2018, August 21). Latest in back-to-school tech: Panic buttons for teachers. *Education Week*. Retrieved from: https://enseo.com/articles/2018/08/21/education-week-latest-in-back-to-school-tech-panic-buttons-for-teachers.

Jones, C. M. (2021, August 1). Schools to add security with the panic alert system. *Florida Times-Union*. Retrieved from: https://jacksonville-fl-app.newsmemory.com/?publink=03abcbacb_1345e95.

More than $83 million school grants now available for school security. (2020, March 23). Securitymagazine.com. Retrieved from: https://www.securitymagazine.com/articles/91967-more-than-83-million-school-grants-now-available-for-school-security.

Perez, Z. (2019, May 13). How are states paying for new school safety measures? Ednote.ecs.org. Retrieved from: https://ednote.ecs.org/how-are-states-paying-for-new-school-safety-measures.

Williams, R., & Deutch, T. (2021, May 21). A bipartisan school safety effort to secure schools. Thehill.com. Retrieved from: https://thehill.com/blogs/congress-blog/politics/554685-a-bipartisan-school-safety-effort-to-secure-schools.

References for Money-Saving Safety Devices—Enthusiasts

Campo-Flores, A. (2020, January 12). Florida considers panic alarms for schools to respond to shootings. *Wall Street Journal*. Retrieved from: https://www.wsj.com/articles/florida-considers-panic-alarms-for-schools-to-respond-to-shootings-11578830400.

Jeffs, A. (2020, April 15). How to thoughtfully implement panic buttons into your school safety plan. *School News*. Retrieved from: https://www.eschoolnews.com/2020/04/15/how-to-thoughtfully-implement-panic-buttons-into-your-school-safety-plan/?all.

Lebron, A. (2020, January 30). Why every school should have a panic button app system. Ravemobilesafety.com. Retrieved from: https://www.ravemobilesafety.com/blog/school-panic-button-app-system-in-an-emergency.

References for Money-Saving Safety Devices—Skeptics

Bloch, E. (2021, July 3). Police look to replace 20 JSO officers. *Florida Times-Union.* Retrieved from: https://jacksonville-fl-app.newsmemory.com/?publink=0349ba9e9_1345e33.

Charles, J. B. (2018, December 13). A growing response to school shootings: Panic buttons on phones. Governing.com. Retrieved from: https://www.governing.com/topics/public-justice-safety/gov-school-shooting-panic-button.html.

Goldstein, D. (2020, June 12). Do police officers make schools safer or more dangerous? *New York Times*. Retrieved from: https://www.nytimes.com/2020/06/12/us/schools-police-resource-officers.html.

Lindsay, C. A., Lee, V., & Lloyd, T. (2018, June 21). The prevalence of police officers in US schools. *Urban Wire.* [Blog]. Retrieved from: https://www.urban.org/urban-wire/prevalence-police-officers-us-schools.

Mamone, M., & Palmer, J. (2019, August 2). Did lobbying efforts influence spending on school panic button? KGOU.org. Retrieved from: https://www.kgou.org/post/did-lobbying-efforts-influence-spending-school-panic-button.

Stern, G., Haynes, S., & Cordero, K. (2019, December 6). In era of school shootings, false alarms create real fear. *Poughkeepsie Journal*. Retrieved from: https://www.poughkeepsiejournal.com/story/news/education/2019/12/06/arlington-lockdown-stemmed-technology-error/4351463002.

CHAPTER 5

References for Chapter 5 Epigraphs

Baldwin, P.—*quoted by* Hajela, A. (2019, October 23). Why police dogs won't be sniffing out drugs in Chapel Hill-Carrboro schools anymore. *News Observer*. Retrieved from: https://www.newsobserver.com/news/local/crime/article236524003.html.

Cervantes, V.—*quoted by* Robles, Y. (2019, May 23). Aurora used drug-sniffing dogs 28 times at schools—And community is asking why. Chalkbeat.org. Retrieved from: https://chalkbeat.org/posts/co/2019/05/23/aurora-used-drug-sniffing-dogs-28-times-at-schools-and-community-is-asking-why.

Flood, R.—*quoted by* Lee, A. (2019, April 15). SC schools deploy drug-sniffing dogs at a cost and with concern, but not from parents. *Greenville News*. Retrieved from: https://www.greenvilleonline.com/story/news/education/2019/04/15/south-carolina-schools-drug-sniffing-dogs-greenville-anderson/3278916002.

Jacobs, M. (2018, March 16). How trained dogs could make schools safer. *News Observer*. Retrieved from: https://www.newsobserver.com/opinion/op-ed/article205485139.html.

Sullivan, L. (2011, June 6). Drug-sniffing dogs in schools make every student a suspect. Aclu-wa.org. Retrieved from: https://www.aclu-wa.org/blog/drug-sniffing-dogs-schools-make-every-student-suspect.

References for Police on Subways—Introduction

Berger, P., & Brody, L. (2019, October 21). Police haven't slowed New Yorkers' subway fare evasion. *Wall Street Journal*. Retrieved from: https://www.wsj.com/articles/police-havent-slowed-new-yorkers-subway-fare-evasion-11571697440.

Fitzsimmons, E. G., & Sandoval, E. (2019, April 13). 1 in 5 bus riders in New York City evades the fare, far worse than elsewhere. *New York Times*. Retrieved from: https://www.nytimes.com/2019/04/13/nyregion/mta-bus-riders-fare-beaters.html.

Meyer, D., & Balsamini, D. (2021, February 13). Calls for more cops on NYC subway grow louder following A train carnage. *New York Post*. Retrieved from: https://nypost.com/2021/02/13/calls-for-more-cops-on-nyc-subway-grow-after-a-train-carnage.

New York City Government. (2020). Transit. Author. Retrieved from: https://www1.nyc.gov/site/nypd/bureaus/transit-housing/transit.page.

Subway fare beaters are costing New York City millions. (2019, February 5). Insideedition.com. Retrieved from: https://www.insideedition.com/subway-fare-beaters-are-costing-new-york-city-millions-so-inside-edition-decided-confront-them.

References for Police on Subways—Enthusiasts

Mosley, T., & Hagan, A. (2019, December 19). Increased subway policing sparks protest in New York City. Wbur.org. Retrieved from: https://www.wbur.org/hereandnow/2019/12/19/nyc-increased-subway-policing-protests.

New York Post Editorial Board. (2020, February 17). Soaring subway crime is more than enough reason to add more MTA police. *New York Post*. Retrieved from: https://nypost.com/2020/02/17/soaring-subway-crime-is-more-than-enough-reason-to-add-more-mta-police.

Subway commuters avoid paying their fare: Caught on hidden camera. (2019, May 26). *YouTub*e (video). Retrieved from: https://www.youtube.com/watch?v=Fhqlh_Q3IFE.

References for Police on Subways—Skeptics

Aratani, L. (2020, February 1). "How do you spell racist? NYPD": New Yorkers protest growing police action on subways. *Guardian*. Retrieved from: https://www.theguardian.com/us-news/2020/feb/01/new-york-city-subway-policing-protests-grand-central.

Chapman, B., & Blint-Welsh, T. (2020, January 31). Protests of policing in New York City subway lead to arrests. *Wall Street Journal*. Retrieved from: https://www

.wsj.com/articles/protests-of-policing-in-new-york-city-subway-lead-to-arrests-11580521991.

Liebson, R. (2019, December 19). Why 500 more officers will police the subway. *New York Times*. Retrieved from: https://www.nytimes.com/2019/12/19/nyregion/mta-subway-police.html.

Thomas, T., Burke, K., & Parascandola, R. (2020, January 31). Protesters vandalize NYC train stations, set off smoke bomb, jump turnstiles in rally against over-policing in subways. *New York Daily News*. Retrieved from: https://www.nydailynews.com/new-york/nyc-crime/ny-nypd-prepares-for-massive-protest-in-nyc-20200131-ksszmcdc2bawfpyrp3bp7d5kbe-story.html.

References for Dogs at School—Introduction

FindLaw Editors. (2020). Using drug-sniffing dogs and canine units. Findlaw.com. Retrieved from: https://education.findlaw.com/student-rights/using-drug-sniffing-dogs-and-canine-units.html.

Russo, C. J. (2013, September). Sniff dogs in schools: Do the noses know? Educational Leadership Faculty Publications, #148. Retrieved from: https://ecommons.udayton.edu/eda_fac_pub/148.

Wisely, J. (2019, May 6). Michigan schools are hiring these dogs to help prevent shootings. *Detroit Free Press*. Retrieved from: https://www.freep.com/story/news/education/2019/05/06/school-shooting-dog-gun-powder/3578897002.

References for Dogs at School—Enthusiasts

3DK9. (2020). Schools. Drugdetectingdogs.com. Retrieved from https://www.drugdetectingdogs.com/schools-drug-sniff-detection-k9.

Firearm detection dog procedures headed toward approval for Chatham schools. (2019, January 25). *Chatham News & Record*. Retrieved from: https://www.chathamnewsrecord.com/stories/firearm-detection-dog-procedures-headed-toward-approval-for-chatham-schools,1495?

Michor, M. (2019, January). Clark County school police welcome dogs trained to detect guns. *Las Vegas Review-Journal*. Retrieved from: https://www.reviewjournal.com/local/education/clark-county-school-police-welcome-dogs-trained-to-detect-guns-1581278/.

Thornton, W. (2015, October 9). Ala. schools use gun-sniffing dogs to find threats. Policeone.com. Retrieved from: https://www.policeone.com/k-9/articles/ala-schools-use-gun-sniffing-dogs-to-find-threats-i02Pa4p2afui5sB7.

Wisely, J. (2019, May 6). Michigan schools are hiring these dogs to help prevent shootings. *Detroit Free Press*. Retrieved from: https://www.freep.com/story/news/education/2019/05/06/school-shooting-dog-gun-powder/3578897002.

References for Dogs at School—Skeptics

Hearing today on expelling teens with knives. (2016, February 11). *San Diego Union-Tribune*. Retrieved from: https://www.sandiegouniontribune.com/news/education/sdut-escondido-knives-dogs-drug-sniffing-2016feb11-story.html.

Kesling, B. (2019, December 24). Who's a good boy? *Wall Street Journal*. Retrieved from: *Wall Street Journal*. Retrieved from: https://www.wsj.com/articles/whos-a-good-boy-police-departments-step-up-training-to-find-which-dogs-are-11577192400.

Rutherford, F. (2015, September 25). Police tried to train sniffer dogs to detect knives. Buzzfeed.com. Retrieved from: https://www.buzzfeed.com/fionarutherford/the-met-commissioner-tried-to-find-out-if-dogs-could-be-used.

Thompson, D. (2021, June 6). Calif. assault weapons ban nixed. *Florida Times-Union*. Retrieved from: https://jacksonville-fl-app.newsmemory.com/?publink=2543c2d5f_1345dd2.

Williamson, E. (2019, September 4). When active-shooter drills scare the children they hope to protect. *New York Times*. Retrieved from: https://www.nytimes.com/2019/09/04/us/politics/active-shooter-drills-schools.html.

CHAPTER 6

References for Chapter 6 Epigraphs

Egenes, L. (2018, May 10). It's time to prevent school violence with meditation—and here's how. Elephantjournal.com. Retrieved from: https://www.elephantjournal.com/now/its-time-to-prevent-school-violence-with-meditation-and-heres-how.

Jaramillo, S.—*quoted by* Wong, A. (2018, September 20). Why schools are banning yoga. *Atlantic*. Retrieved from: https://www.theatlantic.com/education/archive/2018/09/why-schools-are-banning-yoga/570904.

Marie, D.—*quoted by* Prafder, E. (2017). Bully-proofing our schools through yoga. Gaiam.com. Retrieved from: https://www.gaiam.com/blogs/discover/bully-proofing-our-schools-through-yoga.

Shanti, W. (2017). Encouraging an end to violence through yoga & meditation. Yogadigest.com. Retrieved from: https://yogadigest.com/encouraging-end-violence-meditation-yoga-meditation.

Singh, K. (2013, January 15). Could yoga for kids reduce violence? Aurawellnesscenter.com. Retrieved from: https://www.aurawellnesscenter.com/2013/01/15/could-yoga-for-kids-reduce-violence.

Strauss, E. (2016, March 2). Being mindful about mindfulness. *Slate*. Retrieved from: https://slate.com/human-interest/2016/03/teaching-mindfulness-meditation-in-schools-a-skeptics-investigation.html.

References for An Unusual Burger—Introduction

Bunge, J. (2020, February 27). Beyond Meat is pushing back against criticism that plant-based products are laden with artificial ingredients. *Wall Street Journal*. Retrieved from: https://www.wsj.com/articles/beyond-meat-plans-to-tout-healthfulness-of-its-burgers-11582837921.

Creswell, J. (2021, September 9). Plant-based foods expand, with consumers hungry for more. *New York Times*. Retrieved from: https://www.nytimes.com/2021/09/08/business/plant-based-food-companies.html.

Moskin, J., Plumer, B., Lieberman, R., & Weingart, E. (2019, April 30). Your questions about food and climate change answered. *New York Times*. Retrieved from: https://www.nytimes.com/interactive/2019/04/30/dining/climate-change-food-eating-habits.html.

Popular and versatile—Ground beef reigns! (2019, April 11). Beefitswhatsfordinner.com. Retrieved from: https://www.beefitswhatsfordinner.com/retail/sales-data-shopper-insights/ground-beef-sales.

Wall Street Journal. (2019, August 13). The $800 million meatless meat industry is just heating up. *Wall Street Journal* (video). Retrieved from: https://www.wsj.com/video/the-800-million-meatless-meat-industry-is-just-heating-up/14C93AEC-790C-4BF4-82D8-225C26CEDDCD.html.

Yaffe-Bellany, D. (2019, October 14). The new makers of plant-based meat: Big meat companies. *New York Times*. Retrieved from: https://www.nytimes.com/2019/10/14/business/the-new-makers-of-plant-based-meat-big-meat-companies.html.

References for An Unusual Burger—Enthusiasts

Lowrey. A. (2019, September 23). What's different about the Impossible Burger? *Atlantic*. Retrieved from: https://www.theatlantic.com/ideas/archive/2019/09/vegan-food-goes-mainstream/598558.

Moskin, J. (2019, October 22). How do the new plant-based burgers stack up? We taste-tested them. *New York Times*. Retrieved from: https://www.nytimes.com/2019/10/22/dining/veggie-burger-taste-test.html.

Santos-Neves, C. (2021). Veggie burger taste test. Epicurious.com. Retrieved from: https://www.epicurious.com/archive/everydaycooking/tastetests/veggieburgertastetest.

We taste-tested top-selling veggie burgers—And these are the best. (2018, April 10). Today.com. Retrieved from: https://www.today.com/food/best-veggie-burgers-market-taste-test-t126541.

References for An Unusual Burger—Skeptics

Berman, R. (2019, November 5). "Plant-based meat" is all hat and no cattle. *Wall Street Journal*. Retrieved from: https://www.wsj.com/articles/plant-based-meat-is-all-hat-and-no-cattle-11572997943.

Coggin, W. (2019, November 2). Let them eat steak: Hold the shame, red meat is not bad for you or climate change. *USA TODAY*. Retrieved from: https://www.usatoday.com/story/opinion/2019/11/02/red-meat-flawed-health-climate-claims-new-research-column/4112887002.

Hu, F. B., Otis, B., & McCarthy, G. (2019, August 26). Can plant-based meat alternatives be part of a healthy and sustainable diet? *Journal of the American Medical Association*. Retrieved from: https://jamanetwork.com/journals/jama/fullarticle/2749260.

O'Connor, A. (2019, December 3). Fake meat vs. real meat. *New York Times*. Retrieved from: https://www.nytimes.com/2019/12/03/well/eat/fake-meat-vs-real-meat.html.

References for An Unusual Disciplinary Strategy—Introduction

Alvin, J., & Warwick, A. (2013). *Music therapy for the autistic child*. Oxford, UK: Oxford University Press.

Betts, D. E., & Betts, S. W. (2006). *Yoga for children with autism spectrum disorders: A step-by-step guide for parents and caregivers*. London: Jessica Kingsley.

Carrión, V. G., & Rettger, J. (Eds). (2019). *Applied mindfulness: Approaches in mental health for children and adolescents*. Washington. DC: American Psychiatric Association Publishing.

Ivtzan, I. (Ed). (2020). *Handbook of mindfulness-based programmes: Mindfulness interventions from education to health and therapy*. New York: Oxford.

Karkou, V. (2010). *Arts therapies in schools: Research and practice*. London: Jessica Kingsley.

Malchiodi, C. (2012, December 21). Art as a path of peace in a violent world. *Psychology Today*. Retrieved from: https://www.psychologytoday.com/us/blog/arts-and-health/201212/art-path-peace-in-violent-world.

McDonald, A., Holttum, S., & Drey, N. (2019, July 2). Primary-school-based art therapy: Exploratory study of changes in children's social, emotional and mental health. *International Journal of Art Therapy*. Retrieved from: https://doi.org/10.1080/17454832.2019.1634115.

Safran, D. S. (2002). *Art therapy and AD/HD: Diagnostic and therapeutic approaches*. London: Jessica Kingsley.

Tomlinson, J., Derrington, P., & Oldfield, A. (2012). *Music therapy in schools: Working with children of all ages in mainstream and special education*. Philadelphia: Jessica Kingsley.

Williams, N. (2010). *Yoga therapy for every special child: Meeting needs in a natural setting*. London: Singing Dragon.

References for An Unusual Disciplinary Strategy—Enthusiasts

Brown, C. G. (2020). *Debating yoga and mindfulness in public schools: Reforming secular education or reestablishing religion*? Chapel Hill: The University of North Carolina Press.

Conboy, L. A., Noggle, J., Frey, J. L., Kudesia, R. S., & Khalsa, B. (2013, May–June). Qualitative evaluation of a high school yoga program: Feasibility and perceived benefits. National Institute of Health. Retrieved from: https://pubmed.ncbi.nlm.nih.gov/23643372.

Frank, J. L., Bose, B., & Schrobenhauser-Clonan, A. (2014, February 14). Effectiveness of a school-based yoga program on adolescent mental health, stress coping strategies, and attitudes toward violence: Findings from a high-risk sample. *Journal of Applied School Psychology*. Retrieved from: https://doi.org/10.1080/15377903.2013.863259.

Hill, M. (2019, May 17). How schools can ward off anxiety, misbehavior and even violence through mindfulness. Njspotlight.com. Retrieved from: https://www.njspotlight.com/news/video/how-schools-can-ward-off-anxiety-misbehavior-and-even-violence-through-mindfulness.

McGinn, M. (2018, October 7). Commentary: Yoga and meditation can make schools less violent. *Salt Lake City Tribune*. Retrieved from: https://www.sltrib.com/opinion/commentary/2018/10/07/commentary-yoga.

Proulx, N. (2019, February 7). Should schools teach mindfulness? *New York Times*. Retrieved from: https://www.nytimes.com/2019/02/07/learning/should-schools-teach-mindfulness.html.

Rosenfeld, J. (2016, January 12). Yoga, but affordable. *Atlantic*. Retrieved from: https://www.theatlantic.com/business/archive/2016/01/yoga-expensive-affordable/423549.

Santas, D. (2016, May 10). Beyond "Namaste": The benefits of yoga in schools. Cnn.com. Retrieved from: https://www.cnn.com/2016/05/10/health/yoga-in-schools/index.html.

Sarkissian, M., Trent, N. L., Huchting, K., & Khalsa, S.B. (2018). Effects of a Kundalini Yoga program on elementary and middle school students' stress, affect, and resilience. *Journal of Developmental and Behavioral Pediatrics*. Retrieved from: https://journals.lww.com/jrnldbp/Abstract/2018/04000/Effects_of_a_Kundalini_Yoga_Program_on_Elementary.4.aspx.

References for An Unusual Disciplinary Strategy—Skeptics

Bloch, E. (2020, December 12). DCPS police lambasted by grand jury report. *Florida Times-Union*. Retrieved from: http://digital.olivesoftware.com/Olive/ODN/FloridaTimesUnion/shared/ShowArticle.aspx?doc=TFTU%2F2020%2F12%2F12&entity=Ar00101&sk=82D632D2&mode=text.

Butzer, B., & Flynn, L. (2018, November 20). Seven ways that yoga is good for schools. Berkeley.edu. Retrieved from: https://greatergood.berkeley.edu/article/item/seven_ways_that_yoga_is_good_for_schools.

Devarajan, K. (2020, January 17). How "Namaste" flew away from us. Npr.org. Retrieved from: https://www.npr.org/sections/codeswitch/2020/01/17/406246770/how-namaste-flew-away-from-us.

Kamenetz, A. (2020, February 27). Schools are embracing mindfulness, but practice doesn't always make perfect. Npr.org. Retrieved from: https://www.npr.org/2020

/02/27/804971750/schools-are-embracing-mindfulness-but-practice-doesnt-always-make-perfect.

Wong, A. (2018, September 20). Why schools are banning yoga. *Atlantic*. Retrieved from: https://www.theatlantic.com/education/archive/2018/09/why-schools-are-banning-yoga/570904.

CHAPTER 7

References for Chapter 7 Epigraphs

Castro, D. (2020, February, 23). Despite the cries of alarm, the technology is mostly beneficial. *Wall Street Journal*. Retrieved from: https://www.wsj.com/articles/should-government-halt-the-use-of-facial-recognition-technology-11582513260.

Ramos, O.—*quoted by* O'Brien, M. (2019, December 18). Why some cities and states balk at face recognition tech. Usnews.com. Retrieved from: https://www.usnews.com/news/business/articles/2019-12-17/why-some-cities-and-states-balk-at-face-recognition-tech.

Shultz, J. (2019, June 7). Facial recognition software. *New York Times*. Retrieved from: https://www.nytimes.com/2019/06/07/opinion/lockport-facial-recognition-schools.html.

Whittaker, M. (2020, February 23). The technology is both biased and prone to errors. *Wall Street Journal*. Retrieved from: https://www.wsj.com/articles/should-government-halt-the-use-of-facial-recognition-technology-11582513260.

References for Error-Prone Loans—Introduction

Eisen, B., & Andriotis, A. (2019, December 21). An $809 car payment, a $660 income: How dealers make the math work. *Wall Street Journal*. Retreived from https://www.wsj.com/articles/an-809-car-payment-a-660-income-how-dealers-make-the-math-work-11576924201.

Weliver, D. (2020, August 27). Why it's so hard to pay off your car loan early (and how to do it anyway). Moneyunder30.com. Retrieved from: https://www.moneyunder30.com/pay-off-your-car-loan-early.

References for Error-Prone Loans—Enthusiasts

Andriotis, A., Brown, K., & Shifflett, S. (2019. August 1). Families go deep in debt to stay in the middle class. *Wall Street Journal*. Retrieved from: https://www.wsj.com/articles/families-go-deep-in-debt-to-stay-in-the-middle-class-11564673734.

Wollenhaupt, G. (2020, April 30). Should I pay off my car loan early? Lendingtree.com. Retrieved from: https://www.lendingtree.com/auto/refinance/car-loans/pay-off-car-loan-early.

References for Error-Prone Loans—Skeptics

Andriotis, A., & Eisen, B. (2019, November 9). A $45,000 loan for a $27,000 ride: More borrowers are going underwater on car loans. *Wall Street Journal*. Retrieved from: https://www.wsj.com/articles/a-45-000-loan-for-a-27-000-ride-more-borrowers-are-going-underwater-on-car-loans-11573295400.

Eisen, B., & Roberts, A. (2019, October 1). The seven-year auto loan: America's middle class can't afford its cars. *Wall Street Journal*. Retrieved from: https://www.wsj.com/articles/the-seven-year-auto-loan-americas-middle-class-cant-afford-their-cars-11569941215.

References for Error-Prone Software—Introduction

Deeks, A., & Mercer, S. T. (2018, March 27). Facial recognition software: Costs and benefits. Lawfareblog.com. Retrieved from: https://www.lawfareblog.com/facial-recognition-software-costs-and-benefits.

Roc Facial Recognition. (2020). Rank One Computing. Retrieved from: https://www.rankone.io/?gclid=Cj0KCQiAoab_BRCxARIsANMx4S5cSA8Jty8RPqlpJW3NqoUk2eKobKuL4rJqoYF2rCKR4F9tD6vi92waAp0aEALw_wcB.

References for Error-Prone Software—Enthusiasts

Ropek, L. (2019, October 17). Facial recognition software on the rise in U.S. schools. Govtech.com. Retrieved from: https://www.govtech.com/products/Facial-Recognition-Software-on-the-Rise-in-US-Schools.html.

Vance, M. (2019, April 1). How facial recognition can provide secure access for k-12 schools. Campuslifesecurity.com. Retrieved from: https://campuslifesecurity.com/articles/2019/04/01/how-facial-recognition-can-provide-secure-access-for-k-12-schools.aspx?

References for Error-Prone Software—Skeptics

Conger, K., Fausset, R., & Kovaleski, S. F. (2019, May 14). San Francisco bans facial recognition technology. *New York Times*. Retrieved from: https://www.nytimes.com/2019/05/14/us/facial-recognition-ban-san-francisco.html.

Engle, J. (2020, February 7). Should facial recognition technology be used in schools? *New York Times*. Retrieved from: https://www.nytimes.com/2020/02/07/learning/should-facial-recognition-technology-be-used-in-schools.html.

O'Brien, M. (2019, December 18). Why some cities and states balk at face recognition tech. Usnews.com. Retrieved from: https://www.usnews.com/news/business/articles/2019-12-17/why-some-cities-and-states-balk-at-face-recognition-tech.

CHAPTER 8

References for Chapter 8 Epigraphs

Barbot, M.—*quoted by* Brody, L. (2020, January 9). New York City's school disciplinary approach ties principals' hands, union says. *Wall Street Journal.* Retrieved from: https://www.wsj.com/articles/new-york-citys-school-disciplinary-approach-ties-principals-hands-union-says-11578615411.

Cardet-Hernandez, B. (2019, June 27). Restorative justice works: I've seen it up close. *New York Daily News*. Retrieved from: https://www.nydailynews.com/opinion/ny-oped-restorative-justice-works-20190627-s6m7dfxguffo5ccv3ndtqdkcpm-story.html.

Center for Court Innovation. (2021). Restorative justice in schools. Courtinnovation.org. Retrieved from: https://www.courtinnovation.org/restorative-justice-schools.

Cuomo, A.—*quoted by* Shea, T. (2020, September 30). Cuomo's NYC recovery plan includes schools, crime—and nat'l guard picking up trash? Nbcnewyork.com. Retrieved from: https://www.nbcnewyork.com/news/local/cuomos-recovery-plan-for-nyc-includes-schools-crime-and-national-guard-cleaning-up-trash/2643284.

DiNapoli, T. (2019, August). *New York State school safety: A statewide and regional review*. Osc.state.ny. Retrieved from: https://www.osc.state.ny.us/files/local-government/publications/pdf/nys-school-safety-statewide-regional-review.pdf.

References for Adapted Tests—Introduction

Giordano, G. (2005). *How testing came to dominate American schools: The history of educational assessment*. New York: Peter Lang.

Giordano, G. (2016). *Common sense questions about tests: The answers can reveal essential steps for improvement*. Lanham, MD: Rowman & Littlefield.

Hartocollis, A., Taylor, K., & Saul, S. (2021, January 19). Retooling during pandemic, the SAT will drop essay and subject tests. *New York Times*. Retrieved from: https://www.nytimes.com/2021/01/19/us/sat-essay-subject-tests.html.

Most U.S. colleges have dropped ACT/SAT requirement for fall 2021 admission. (2020, June 26). Georgetown.edu. Retrieved from: https://feed.georgetown.edu/access-affordability/most-u-s-colleges-have-dropped-act-sat-requirement-for-fall-2021-admission/#:~:text=More%20than%201%2C240%20of%20the,%26%20Open%20Testing%20(FairTest).

Riccards, M. P. (2010). *The College Board and American higher education*. Madison, NJ: Fairleigh Dickinson University Press.

References for Adapted Tests—Enthusiasts

Giordano, G. (2015). *Commonsense questions about school administrators: The answers can reveal essential steps for improvement*. Lanham, MD: Rowman & Littlefield.

Hobbs, T. D. (2019, September 24). SAT scores fall as more students take the test. *Wall Street Journal*. Retrieved from: https://www.wsj.com/articles/the-sat-and-act-have-issues-here-are-three-ideas-to-replace-the-college-admissions-tests-11628348401?mod=hp_listc_pos2.

Korn, M. (2021, August 7). The SAT and ACT have issues. *Wall Street Journal*. Retrieved from: https://www.wsj.com/articles/the-sat-and-act-have-issues-here-are-three-ideas-to-replace-the-college-admissions-tests-11628348401?mod=hp_listc_pos2.

References for Adapted Tests—Skeptics

Belkin, D. (2019, August 27). College Board drops plans for SAT student adversity scores. *Wall Street Journal*. Retrieved from: https://www.wsj.com/articles/college-board-drops-plans-for-sat-student-adversity-scores-11566928181.

Belkin, D. (2019, November 26). What happens if SAT scores consider adversity? *Wall Street Journal*. Retrieved from: https://www.wsj.com/articles/what-happens-if-sat-scores-consider-adversity-11574773201.

Belkin, D. (2020, May 21). University of California will stop using SAT, ACT. *Wall Street Journal*. Retrieved from: https://www.wsj.com/articles/what-happens-if-sat-scores-consider-adversity-11574773201.

Wall Street Journal Editorial Board. (2019, August 27). The SAT changes its answer. *Wall Street Journal*. Retrieved from: https://www.wsj.com/articles/the-sat-changes-its-answer-11566948554.

References for Adapted Discipline—Introduction

Emling, D. (2020). *Institutional racism and restorative justice: Oppression and privilege in America*. New York: Routledge.

Gardner, T. (2016). *Discipline over punishment: Successes and struggles with restorative justice in schools*. Lanham, Maryland: Rowman & Littlefield.

Wadhwa, A. (2017). *Restorative justice in urban schools: Disrupting the school-to-prison pipeline*. New York: Routledge.

References for Adapted Discipline—Enthusiasts

Harris, R. (2020, September 25). This is the casual racism that I face at my elite high school. *New York Times*. Retrieved from: https://www.nytimes.com/2020/09/24/nyregion/regis-catholic-school-racism.html.

Wall Street Journal Editorial Board. (2019, October 17). Chicago teachers strike again. *Wall Street Journal*. Retrieved from: https://www.wsj.com/articles/chicago-teachers-strike-again-11571353385.

References for Adapted Discipline—Skeptics

Barshay, J. (2019, May 6). The promise of "restorative justice" starts to falter under rigorous research. *Hechinger Report*. Retrieved from: https://hechingerreport.org/the-promise-of-restorative-justice-starts-to-falter-under-rigorous-research.

Brody, L. (2020, January 9). New York City's school disciplinary approach ties principals' hands, union says. *Wall Street Journal*. Retrieved from: https://www.wsj.com/articles/new-york-citys-school-disciplinary-approach-ties-principals-hands-union-says-11578615411.

Elsen-Rooney, M. (2020, January 9). Few NYC school administrators satisfied with changes to discipline code: Principals union. *New York Daily News*. Retrieved from: https://www.nydailynews.com/new-york/education/ny-student-discipline-principals-20200109-u7rdk7xwozbddcnbo6peo424wu-story.html.

CHAPTER 9

References for Chapter 9 Epigraphs

American Psychological Association. (2021). Bullying. Author. Retrieved from: https://www.apa.org/topics/bullying.

Missouri State Statute §160.775. (2016). Anti-bullying policy required: Missouri Revised Statutes §160.775. Author. Retrieved from: https://revisor.mo.gov/main/OneSection.aspx?section=160.775&bid=33227&hl=.

Southern California American Civil Liberties Union. (2021). SETH'S LAW (AB9)—Your right to not be bullied at school. Author. Retrieved from: https://www.aclusocal.org/en/seths-law.

Temkin, D.—*quoted by* Arzate, H. A. (2019, September 3). In battle against bullies, some schools target parents. *Education Week*. Retrieved from: https://www.edweek.org/leadership/in-battle-against-bullies-some-schools-target-parents/2019/09.

U.S. Department of Health and Human Services. (2021a). Florida anti-bullying laws & policies. Retrieved from: https://www.stopbullying.gov/resources/laws/florida.

U.S. Department of Health and Human Services. (2021b). Get help now. Retrieved from: https://www.stopbullying.gov/resources/get-help-now.

References for Availability Bias Affects Tourists—Introduction

Agarwal, P. (2019, July 29). Availability bias. Intelligenteconomist.com. Retrieved from: https://www.intelligenteconomist.com/availability-bias.

Holly, A. (2019, July 25). Why Florida is lightning-capital-of-the-United States. Wfla.com. Retrieved from: https://www.wfla.com/weather/florida-lightning-capital-of-the-united-states.

Miller, K. (2021, August 4). In July, 2 dead, 3 injured on Florida's southwest coast from lightning. *Florida Times-Union*. Retrieved from: https://jacksonville-fl-app.newsmemory.com/?publink=066ffbc21_1345e98.

Sarkis, S. A. (2020, June 27). Here, there, and everywhere: How availability bias messes up your relationships. *Psychology Today*. Retrieved from: https://www.psychologytoday.com/us/blog/here-there-and-everywhere/202006/how-availability-bias-messes-your-relationships.

Sosnowski, A. (2021). Why Florida ranks highest for lightning fatalities in the US. Accuweather.com. Retrieved from: https://www.accuweather.com/en/weather-news/why-florida-ranks-highest-for-lightning-fatalities-in-the-us/350561#:~:text=While%20Florida%20is%20known%20as,year%20study%20according%20to%20Vaisala.

References for Availability Bias Affects Tourists—Enthusiasts

Florida State Golf Association. (2018, June 1). Rules of golf—Florida's challenging weather. Author. Retrieved from: https://www.fsga.org/News/Details/1442.

Killer, E. (2020, February 11). Shark season officially underway in South Florida. Tcpalm.com. Retrieved from: https://www.tcpalm.com/story/news/local/florida/2020/02/11/sharks-closer-florida-beachgoers-than-you-think-time-year/4721989002.

Lightning prediction vs. lightning detection for golf courses. (2019, April 12). Earthnetworks.com. Retrieved from: https://www.earthnetworks.com/blog/lightning-prediction-vs-detection-golf/.

Miller, K. (2016, August 29). Truths and myths about summer lightning and golf in South Florida. *Palm Beach Post*. Retrieved from: https://www.palmbeachpost.com/article/20150904/NEWS/812069495.

Tracking sharks (2021). Author. Retrieved from: https://www.trackingsharks.com.

What are the odds of being struck by lightning in the US? (2021). Bestuscasinos.org. Retrieved from: https://www.bestuscasinos.org/blog/odds-of-being-struck-by-lightning-in-the-us.

References for Availability Bias Affects Tourists—Skeptics

Giordano, C. (2020, April 18). 20 reasons not to move to Florida. Toughnickel.com. Retrieved from: https://toughnickel.com/real-estate/20-Reasons-Not-to-Move-to-Florida.

References for Availability Bias Affects Parents—Introduction

Campbell, M., & Bauman, S. (2018). *Reducing cyberbullying in schools: International evidence-based best practices*. London, United Kingdom: Academic Press.

Johnson, J. (2021, February 10). Cyber bullying—Statistics & facts. Statista.com. Retrieved from: https://www.statista.com/topics/1809/cyber-bullying.

Redd, A. (2019, May 22). My child was being bullied at school—Here's what I did and what you can do, too. *Washington Post*. Retrieved from: https://www

.washingtonpost.com/lifestyle/2019/05/17/my-child-was-being-bullied-school-heres-what-i-did-what-you-can-do-too.

U. S. Department of Health and Human Services. (2021c). Report cyberbullying to law enforcement. Retrieved from: https://www.stopbullying.gov/cyberbullying/how-to-report.

U.S. Secret Service. (2019). *Protecting America's schools: A U.S. Secret Service analysis of targeted school violence*. U.S. Secret Service. Retrieved from: https://www.secretservice.gov/sites/default/files/2020-04/Protecting_Americas_Schools.pdf.

References for Availability Bias Affects Parents—Enthusiasts

Bradshaw, C. P., & Waasdorp, T. E. (2020). *Preventing bullying in schools: A social and emotional learning approach to prevention and early intervention*. New York: Norton.

England, D. C. (2021). Cyberbullying laws in California. Criminaldefenselawyer.com. Retrieved from: https://www.criminaldefenselawyer.com/resources/cyberbullying-laws-california.htm.

Hatzenbuehler, M. L., Schwab-Reese, L., Ranapurwala, S. I., et al. (2015, October 5). Associations between antibullying policies and bullying in 25 states. *JAMA Pediatrics*. Retrieved from: https://jamanetwork.com/journals/jamapediatrics/article-abstract/2442853.

National Threat Assessment Center (U.S.). (2019). Protecting America's schools: A U.S. Secret Service analysis of targeted school violence. (Washington, D.C.): U.S. Department of Homeland Security, United States Secret Service, National Threat Assessment Center, 2019. Retrieved from: https://www.secretservice.gov/sites/default/files/2020-04/Protecting_Americas_Schools.pdf.

References for Availability Bias Affects Parents—Skeptics

Koh, Y., & Smith, R. A. (2021, June 29). Schools weigh discipline after supreme court ruling on student speech. *Wall Street Journal*. Retrieved from: https://www.wsj.com/articles/schools-weigh-discipline-after-supreme-court-ruling-on-student-speech-11625000207.

Twemlow, S. W., & Sacco, F. C. (2008). *Why school antibullying programs don't work*. Lanham, MD: Aronson.

CHAPTER 10

References for Chapter 10 Epigraphs

Basra, V., & Patino-Lydia, V. (2020, February 23). Too many girls are Baker Acted. *Florida Times-Union*. Retrieved from: http://digital.olivesoftware.com/Olive/ODN

/FloridaTimesUnion/shared/ShowArticle.aspx?doc=TFTU%2F2020%2F02%2F23&entity=Ar03302&sk=514A4C4A&mode=text.

Caskey, H.—*quoted by* Gluck, F. (2019, August 21). Florida kids are getting sent to psychiatric units under the Baker Act in record numbers. News-press.com. Retrieved from: https://www.news-press.com/in-depth/news/2019/08/21/florida-children-baker-act-record-numbers-mental-health/3247904002.

Falk, M.—*quoted by* Bloch, E. (2020, February 14). Girl held for evaluation "pleasant," calm. *Florida Times-Union*. Retrieved from: http://digital.olivesoftware.com/Olive/ODN/FloridaTimesUnion/shared/ShowArticle.aspx?doc=TFTU%2F2020%2F02%2F14&entity=Ar00101&sk=A9EBBA33&mode=text.

Hatter, L. (2020, December 14). About the data—Committed: Children and the Baker Act. Wusf.usf.edu. Retrieved from: https://wusfnews.wusf.usf.edu/health-news-florida/2020-12-15/about-the-data-committed-children-and-the-baker-act.

School District of Lee County. (2021). Baker Act. School District of Lee County Mental Health and Wellness Portal. Retrieved from: https://www.leeschools.net/student_services/mental_health_and_wellness_portal/baker_act.

Weaver, T. (2021). Baker Act patients need rights. *Florida Times-Union*. Retrieved from: https://jacksonville-fl-app.newsmemory.com/?publink=23d743b9a_1345d78.

References for Strict Library Fines—Introduction

American Library Association. (2014, November). Fines and overdues. Author. Retrieved from: http://www.ala.org/tools/atoz/fines-and-overdues.

References for Strict Library Fines—Enthusiasts

Morehart, P. (2018, June 1). Two takes on the library-fine debate: An overdue discussion. *American Libraries Magazine*. Retrieved from: https://americanlibrariesmagazine.org.

References for Strict Library Fines—Skeptics

Bowman, E. (2019, November 30). We wanted our patrons back—Public libraries scrap late fines to alleviate inequity. NPR.org. Retrieved from: https://www.npr.org/2019/11/30/781374759/we-wanted-our-patrons-back-public-libraries-scrap-late-fines-to-alleviate-inequi.

Coelho, S. (2020, January 30). Library fines are trash and people are taking notice. Bookriot.com. Retrieved from: https://bookriot.com/fine-free-libraries-trend.

Reed, K., Blackburn, J., & Sifton, D. (2014, May). Putting a sacred cow out to pasture: Assessing the removal of fines and reduction of barriers at a small academic library. *Journal of Academic Librarianship*. Retrieved from: https://www.sciencedirect.com/science/article/pii/S0099133314000573.

Ross, T. (2019, February 27). Not so fine with library fines: A look at the overdue debate. Ebsco.com. Retrieved from: https://www.ebsco.com/blogs/ebscopost/not-so-fine-library-fines-look-overdue-debate.

Washington Post Editorial Board. (2018, June 17). More libraries are going fine-free: That's good for everyone. *Washington Post*. Retrieved from: https://www.washingtonpost.com/opinions/2018/06/15/7ad6f80e-709d-11e8-afd5-778aca903bbe_story.html.

References for Strict Psychiatric Detentions and Screenings—Introduction

Forman, S. G. (2015). *Implementation of mental health programs in schools: A change agent's guide*. Washington, DC: American Psychological Association.

Gibson, T. (2019, July 18). Florida mandates mental health training for students in grades 6–12. *Education Week*. Retrieved from: https://www.edweek.org/leadership/florida-mandates-mental-health-training-for-students-in-grades-6-12/2019/07.

Kamp, J., & Calvert, S. (2018, February 15). Gunman kills 17 in Florida high school shooting. *Wall Street Journal*. Retrieved from https://www.wsj.com/articles/shooting-at-florida-high-school-authorities-report-1518638881.

Ketterer, W. (2020). *Reducing anger and violence in schools: An evidence-based approach*. New York, NY: Routledge.

Weist, M. D., Lever, N. A., Bradshaw, C. P., & Owens, J. S. (2014). *Handbook of school mental health: Research, training, practice, and policy*. New York: Springer.

References for Strict Psychiatric Detentions and Screenings—Enthusiasts

Basics of the Florida Baker Act. (2020, February 21). Thomsonreuters.com. Retrieved from: https://legal.thomsonreuters.com/blog/basics-of-the-florida-baker-act.

Healey, K. (2019, October 1). 9 facts: History of Florida's Baker Act law. WFTV.com. Retrieved from: https://www.wftv.com/news/local/9-facts-history-of-florida-s-baker-act-law/992247631.

References for Strict Psychiatric Detentions and Screenings—Skeptics

Bloch, E. (2020, February 14). Girl held for evaluation "pleasant," calm. *Florida Times-Union*. Retrieved from: http://digital.olivesoftware.com/Olive/ODN/FloridaTimesUnion/shared/ShowArticle.aspx?doc=TFTU%2F2020%2F02%2F14&entity=Ar00101&sk=A9EBBA33&mode=text.

Ceballos, A. (2020, March 5). House passes school safety bill. *Florida Times-Union*. Retrieved from: *http://digital.olivesoftware.com/Olive/ODN/FloridaTimesUnion/shared/ShowArticle.aspx?doc=TFTU%2F2020%2F03%2F05&entity=Ar01104&sk=644F5505&mode=text*.

Florida Times-Union Editorial Board. (2015, November 6). Florida's Baker Act is overused, inefficient and inadequate. *Florida Times-Union*. Retrieved from: https://www.jacksonville.com/article/20151106/opinion/801256697.

Florida Times-Union Editorial Board. (2021, February 16). There's a line between "stupid" and "felony." *Florida Times-Union.* Retrieved from: https://jacksonville-fl-app.newsmemory.com/?publink=0063a9461_1345c4c.

Gluck, F. (2019, August 21). Florida kids are getting sent to psychiatric units under the Baker Act in record numbers. News-press.com. Retrieved from: https://www.news-press.com/in-depth/news/2019/08/21/florida-children-baker-act-record-numbers-mental-health/3247904002.

Hatter, L. (2020, December 14). Committed: Florida's children victims of dysfunctional Baker Act system. Wusf.org. Retrieved from: https://wusf.org/committed-floridas-children-victims-of-dysfunctional-baker-act-system.

Kamp, J., & Calvert, S. (2018, February 15). Gunman kills 17 in Florida high school shooting. *Wall Street Journal*. Retrieved from https://www.wsj.com/articles/shooting-at-florida-high-school-authorities-report-1518638881.

CHAPTER 11

References for Chapter 11 Epigraphs

Ceballos, A. (2019, December 11). The exact number of Florida teachers with guns remains under wraps. *Orlando Weekly*. Retrieved from: https://www.orlandoweekly.com/Blogs/archives/2019/12/11/the-exact-number-of-florida-teachers-with-guns-remains-under-wraps.

Diaz, M.—*quoted by* Ceballos, A. (2019, December 11). The exact number of Florida teachers with guns remains under wraps. *Orlando Weekly*. Retrieved from: https://www.orlandoweekly.com/Blogs/archives/2019/12/11/the-exact-number-of-florida-teachers-with-guns-remains-under-wraps.

Ingram, F.—*quoted by* Mettler, K. (2019, May 9). It's the law now: In Florida, teachers can carry guns at school. *Washington Post*. Retrieved from: https://www.washingtonpost.com/education/2019/05/09/its-law-now-florida-teachers-can-carry-guns-school.

Mettler, K. (2019, May 9). It's the law now: In Florida, teachers can carry guns at school. *Washington Post*. Retrieved from: https://www.washingtonpost.com/education/2019/05/09/its-law-now-florida-teachers-can-carry-guns-school.

Palm Beach Post Editorial Board. (2021, March 25). Fla. lawmakers must wake up to gun violence. *Palm Beach Post.* Retrieved from: https://jacksonville-fl-app.newsmemory.com/?publink=0f1500f9a_1345cb9.

Stokes, S.—*quoted by* Miller, J. (2019, May 10). Teachers blast idea of guns in class after Florida bill becomes law. *New York Post*. Retrieved from: https://nypost.com/2019/05/10/teachers-blast-idea-of-guns-in-class-after-florida-bill-becomes-law.

References for Bonus-Winning Teachers—Introduction

Florida Education Association. (2019, September 23). Best and Brightest update. Florida Education Association. Retrieved from: https://feaweb.org/news/frontline/best-and-brightest-update.

Pinellas County Schools. (2021). Florida's Best and Brightest teacher scholarship program. PCSB.org. Retrieved from: https://www.pcsb.org/Page/16287.

References for Bonus-Winning Teachers—Enthusiasts

Saunders, J. (2019, September 21). Approval sought for "Best and Brightest" settlement. *Florida Times-Union*. Retrieved from: http://digital.olivesoftware.com/Olive/ODN/FloridaTimesUnion/shared/ShowArticle.aspx?doc=TFTU%2F2019%2F09%2F21&entity=Ar01207&sk=B65B7CE7&mode=text.

Wamsley, L. (2019, May 2). Florida approves bill allowing classroom teachers to be armed. NPR.org. Retrieved from: https://www.npr.org/2019/05/02/719585295/florida-approves-bill-allowing-classroom-teachers-to-be-armed.

References for Bonus-Winning Teachers—Skeptics

Ceballos, A. (2019, November 15). Gov. DeSantis: Replace "Best and Brightest" with new teacher bonus plan. WUSF.usf.edu. Retrieved from: https://wusfnews.wusf.usf.edu/education/2019-11-15/gov-desantis-replace-best-and-brightest-with-new-teacher-bonus-plan.

Claire, A. (2016, January 28). Best and Brightest revisions don't cut it, critics say. *Curcio Democra*t. Retrieved from: https://www.tallahassee.com/story/news/2016/01/28/best-and-brightest-revisions-dont-cut-critics-say/79420092.

DeSantis proposes $1,000 bonuses for teachers, principals. (2021, April 3). *Florida Times-Union*. Retrieved from: https://jacksonville-fl-app.newsmemory.com/?publink=2d9cceae2_1345d07.

Nicol, R. (2019, February 13). FEA President: Arming teachers is "wrong conversation." Floridapolitics.com. Retrieved from: https://floridapolitics.com/archives/288224-fea-president-arming-teachers.

Postal, L. (2019, October 1). Florida's "best and brightest"' teachers to get bonuses, but controversial program may soon end. *Orlando Sentinel*. Retrieved from: https://www.orlandosentinel.com/news/education/os-ne-best-brightest-bonuses-teachers-20191001-tupdu2xuwvhcjotaifwyo3x2h4-story.html.

References for Gun-Carrying Teachers—Introduction

Holson, L. M. (2019, October 1). Florida teachers can now carry guns at school. *New York Times*. Retrieved from: https://www.nytimes.com/2019/10/01/us/florida-teachers-guns.html.

Keane, L. (2020, October 8). Number of concealed-carry permit holders near 20 million and growing. *Game and Fish Magazine*. Retrieved from: https://www

.gameandfishmag.com/editorial/concealed-carry-permit-holders-near-20-million-and-growing/385133.

Rajan, S., & Branas, C. C. (2018, June 6). Arming schoolteachers: What do we know? *American Journal of Public Health*. Retrieved from: https://ajph.aphapublications.org/doi/full/10.2105/AJPH.2018.304464.

Should teachers carry guns? (2018, November 28). *Education Week*. Retrieved from: https://www.edweek.org/ew/issues/arming-teachers.html.

References for Gun-Carrying Teachers—Enthusiasts

Mahoney, E. L. (2019, May 1). Classroom teachers can have guns. *Miami Herald*. Retrieved from: https://www.miamiherald.com/news/politics-government/state-politics/article229906419.html.

Swisher, S. (2019, September 17). Most Florida school districts pass on arming teachers, state officials report. *South Florida Sun Sentinel*. Retrieved from: https://www.sun-sentinel.com/news/politics/fl-ne-armed-teachers-update-20190917-entphpzo55bvlmm3me4ue4rkwy-story.html.

References for Gun-Carrying Teachers—Skeptics

Campo-Flores, A. (2019, September 9). Florida decided to let teachers carry guns but few are. *Wall Street Journal*. Retrieved from: https://www.wsj.com/articles/most-florida-schools-opt-out-of-arming-teachers-11568030401.

Miller, J. (2019, May 10). Teachers blast idea of guns in class after Florida bill becomes law. *New York Post*. Retrieved from: https://nypost.com/2019/05/10/teachers-blast-idea-of-guns-in-class-after-florida-bill-becomes-law.

Williams, P. (2021, March 30). Secret Service report says school shootings are preventable, with similar warning signs. NBCnews.com. Retrieved from: https://www.nbcnews.com/politics/politics-news/secret-service-report-says-school-shootings-are-preventable-similar-warning-n1262472.

CHAPTER 12

References for Chapter 12 Epigraphs

Hudson, D. L. (2020). Rap Music and the First Amendment. Middle Tennessee University. Retrieved from: https://www.mtsu.edu/first-amendment/article/1582/rap-music-and-the-first-amendment.

Ryan-Onken, C.—quoted by Brennan, C. (2016, August 24). Parents say Portland district's school bus ban on rap music is racist. *New York Daily News*. Retrieved from: https://www.nydailynews.com/news/national/parents-district-school-bus-ban-rap-music-racist-article-1.2764645.

Westling, C.—*quoted by* Barnes, B. (2016, August 24). Portland Public Schools "rap music" ban sparks allegations of racism. *Oregonian*. Retrieved from: https://www.oregonlive.com/education/2016/08/portland_public_schools_rap_mu.html.

Williams, D. (2019). Should rap music be banned to teenagers because of the influence it causes to teens for violence, sex and drugs? Quora.com. Retrieved from: https://www.quora.com/Should-rap-music-be-banned-to-teenagers-because-of-the-influence-it-causes-to-teens-for-violence-sex-and-drugs.

References for Restricting Corporate Clothing Sales—Introduction

Cerullo, M. (2019, April 3). Patagonia will no longer sell vests with finance firm logos on them. Cbsnews.com. Retrieved from: https://www.cbsnews.com/news/midtown-uniform-patagonia-will-no-longer-sell-vests-with-finance-firms-logos-on-them.

Hemlock, D. (2013, May 27). One percent for the planet: Businesses donate to help the environment. *Sun Sentinel*. Retrieved from: https://www.sun-sentinel.com/business/fl-xpm-2013-05-27-fl-one-percent-planet-20130527-story.html.

We're in business to save our planet. (2021). Activism. Patagonia.com. Retrieved from: https://www.patagonia.com/activism.

References for Restricting Corporate Clothing Sales—Enthusiasts

Blakely, L (2018, November 30). Patagonia's unapologetically political strategy and the massive business it has built. Inc.com. Retrieved from: https://www.inc.com/lindsay-blakely/patagonia-2018-company-of-the-year-nominee.html.

Feldman, J. (2017, January 31). Patagonia just made another major move to save the earth and your wallet. *Huffington Post*. Retrieved from: https://www.huffpost.com/entry/patagonia-return-old-clothes_n_588f8066e4b02772c4e81e8d.

Stevenson, S. (2012, April 26). Patagonia's founder is America's most unlikely business guru. *Wall Street Journal*. Retrieved from: https://www.wsj.com/articles/SB10001424052702303513404577352221465986612.

References for Restricting Corporate Clothing Sales—Skeptics

Another Patagonia-approved wool producer exposed—Help sheep now. (2021). Peta.org. Retrieved from: https://investigations.peta.org/another-patagonia-approved-wool-producer-exposed.

Demkes, E. (2020, April 28). The more Patagonia rejects consumerism, the more the brand sells. Thecorrespondent.com. Retrieved from: https://thecorrespondent.com/424/the-more-patagonia-rejects-consumerism-the-more-the-brand-sells/56126501376-a30f2daa.

Erdmane, A. (2019, July 3). Patagonia's conflicting green consumerism. Commercialwaste.trade. Retrieved from: https://commercialwaste.trade/patagonias

-conflicting-green-consumerism/#:~:text=Back%20in%202015%2C%20Patagonia %20received,only%20concern%20within%20Patagonia's%20products.

References for Restricting Rap Music—Introduction

Barnes, B. (2016, August 24). Portland Public Schools "rap music" ban sparks allegations of racism. *Oregonian*. Retrieved from: https://www.oregonlive.com/education/2016/08/portland_public_schools_rap_mu.html.

Bynoe, Y. (2006). *Encyclopedia of rap and hip-hop culture*. Westport, CN: Greenwood Press.

Campuzano, E. (2019, November 13). Teens in Portland Public Schools say they're not excited about class, feel little connection to staff and faculty. *Oregonian*. Retrieved from: https://www.oregonlive.com/education/2019/11/teens-in-portland-public-schools-say-theyre-not-excited-about-class-feel-little-connection-to-staff-and-faculty.html.

Comnes, J. (2019, October 17). Amid anxiety about school shootings, nine Portland schools ordered unneeded lockdowns in the past 13 months. Wweek.com. Retrieved from: https://www.wweek.com/news/schools/2019/10/16/amid-anxiety-about-school-shootings-nine-portland-schools-ordered-unneeded-lockdowns-in-the-past-13-months.

Connor, M. E., Adams, K., & Zechory, I. (2018). *The musical artistry of rap*. Jefferson, NC: McFarland.

Kajikawa, L. (2015). *Sounding race in rap songs*. Oakland: University of California Press.

Keyes, C. L. (2004). *Rap music and street consciousness*. Urbana: University of Illinois Press.

Ogbar, J. (2007). *Hip-hop revolution: The culture and politics of rap*. Lawrence: University Press of Kansas.

Portland Public Schools Department of Student Transportation. (2009). Student transportation responsibilities. Www.pps.net. Retrieved from: https://www.pps.net/cms/lib/OR01913224/Centricity/Domain/61/Transportation_Guidelines.pdf.

Portland Public Schools. (2021). Threats of violence or harm. Www.pps.net. Retrieved from: https://www.pps.net/Page/1753.

Southern, E. (1997). *The music of black Americans: A history*. New York: Norton.

References for Restricting Rap Music—Enthusiasts

Dunbar, A. (2017, August 7). Rap on trial: Do violent lyrics prove a crime? Thecrimereport.org. Retrieved from: https://thecrimereport.org/2017/08/07/Rap-On-Trial-Do-Violent-Lyrics-Prove-A-Crime.

Portland Public Schools Department of Student Transportation. (2009). Student transportation responsibilities. Pps.net. Retrieved from: https://www.pps.net/cms/lib/OR01913224/Centricity/Domain/61/Transportation_Guidelines.pdf.

References for Restricting Rap Music—Skeptics

Barnes, B. (2016, August 24). Portland Public Schools "rap music" ban sparks allegations of racism. *Oregonian.* Retrieved from: https://www.oregonlive.com/education/2016/08/portland_public_schools_rap_mu.html.

Brennan, C. (2016, August 24). Parents say Portland district's school bus ban on rap music is racist. *New York Daily News.* Retrieved from: https://www.nydailynews.com/news/national/parents-district-school-bus-ban-rap-music-racist-article-1.2764645.

Criminologist says rap music shouldn't be used to incriminate defendants. (2015, December 31). Thecrimereport.org. Retrieved from: https://thecrimereport.org/2015/12/31/2015-12-criminologist-studies-rap.s

Hudson, D. L. (2020). Rap Music and the First Amendment. Middle Tennessee University. Retrieved from: https://www.mtsu.edu/first-amendment/article/1582/rap-music-and-the-first-amendment.

Jones, N. (2020, January 13). Why hip-hop belongs in today's classrooms. Theconversation.com. Retrieved from: http://theconversation.com/why-hip-hop-belongs-in-todays-classrooms-128993.

Lee, L. (2020, February 7). The power of rap and hip-hop in the classroom. Edutopia.org. Retrieved from: https://www.edutopia.org/article/power-rap-and-hip-hop-classroom.

Prakash, N. (2016, August 25). Parents are outraged after Portland public schools banned rap music on their buses. Splinternews.com. Retrieved from: https://splinternews.com/parents-are-outraged-after-portland-public-schools-bann-1793861390.

Weilert, L. (2019, April 9). Schools should not ban music applications. Hayshighguidon.com. Retrieved from: https://hayshighguidon.com/opinion/2019/04/09/schools-should-not-ban-music-applications.

About the Author

Gerard Giordano has been a professor at four universities. He has written eight books examining the questions parents pose about their children's schools. All these books have been published by *Rowman & Littlefield Education.*